GOTTA
STORY
TO
TELL

Thanks for your support! Continue to be "Stronger than the struggle" Dr. Jaclyn Walker

LAKEESHA ATKINSON

LEATHA BALLARD

AMIRA BETHEA

VELVET SMITH

ASHLEY STARLING

DR. JACLYN WALKER

Thanks so much for your support. Many blessings to you

Contents

      References

      Resources/Contact Information

      Book Club Questions

      About the Authors

PREFACE

Anonymous stated, "Never be ashamed of a scar. It simply means you were stronger than whatever tried to hurt you." This quote embodies the essence of the invisible and visible scars that the authors had to endure in their lives.

"Gotta Story to Tell" brought to you by Dr. Jaclyn Walker takes you on a journey of 6 different women that proved to be "stronger than the struggle". These women have survived stories of abuse, drugs, heartache and even suicide and now stand in triumph.

The various journeys that you will be mesmerized by will not only inspire, but empower you to be stronger than your struggle as well. It will also help you to remember that "what doesn't kill you makes you stronger."

MISSING YOU

BY: AMIRA BETHEA

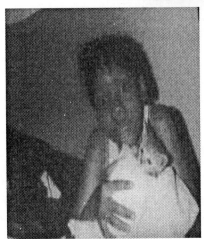

Another day staring out the window. Not admiring the stars or the night sky. Not even looking at the sky to thank the man above at all. There was no need to anymore. I was tired of disappointment time and time again. I'm looking out the window thinking it is another day of "Missing You". Cracked Roads, kids still playing, the view of the wide brownstone steps. Corner stores gated and so many people too, I guess. Yes, the city that never sleeps. The typical New York street, always straight busy no matter what. Life is for everyone no matter what the motive is. But "I'm still missing you". Wishing and hoping you pull up at any time. Even though you didn't acknowledge me when you were around. "I'd look in the sky and ask God, Why he can't look his baby girl in the eye?"

Eight years old seeing things and knowing things that even I knew I shouldn't. Feelings of exhaustion and wanting to give up but still I'm missing you. She came by to pick me and brother up. People on the streets referred to her as many things but we referred to her as mom. I saw her more than pops but that wasn't better. Pops chose the women over us and mom chose her addiction. Thankful for my sister choosing us. Pops chose women which caused mother so many shortcomings. You would think we had a fourth sibling because mother loved her addiction as if it was a fourth child. Giving us money but wanting it back in an hour or so. Sometimes it was quicker than that. Sometimes she wanted the money we would just have on us. Selling her soul is what mother was doing. All she and pops did was run the streets.

The only thing is pops has a full-time job as a postal worker. I would never forget looking through the wall of the abandoned house seeing moms on her knees. The guy's eyes rolling in the back of his head. All I know is that mother didn't look well at all but the guy looked like he was having the time of his life. She would do any and everything for her fourth child. Going back to aunt's house was like going back to an orphanage. Well, should I say nana's house? The only thing I owned was a toothbrush and a dresser drawer, to say the least. I should be grateful God but damn the life I have. Please God "Oh tell me why why-why"? I'm only eight years old. Why do I have to tell myself daily that I am beautiful even though the soles of my shoes are gone? Even though my ponytail is crooked and my hair is so dry and brittle. Even though I have hand me downs on, I should be so grateful.

Why do I have to tell myself, "Hey Moonie (my nickname), you are beautiful" Going to sleep with tears in my eyes feeling like I'm an inmate preparing for survival the next day. Hoping the food I eat is better than yesterday. Hoping that the room temperature is in-between instead of too cold or too hot. Hoping I don't hear the squealing of the mice running through the darkness of the house. Oh, how I wish but that's not happening. No fairy Godmother to come save my rags and turn it to riches. Hot summer day, fire hydrate on blast. I'm having a blast, my t-shirt and shorts are so heavy from the water soaking me. So I sit and start to watch the other kids enjoy themselves. My friends play a while in there nice bathing suits they need no break from the heavy waters of the hydrate because they have on the proper gear. The little things man, the simple things.

I hear my friend's father call her in. She went running and he said to her go take your shower, my beautiful daughter. I started to hate her because I became so jealous of what she had that I wanted so badly. I wish I could live with her but that was impossible. From that day forward I didn't speak to her again. She had what I wanted. Thanks a lot pops for your absence, but I'm still missing you. I will continue to reflect about my pops when I go to bed in my cell.

Time and time again I would think of what it would feel like to have a mother and a father. The white picket fence with everyone looking in. The nice cars in the driveway. Me and my siblings playing outside and then mother calling us in for dinner. The kind of shit you see on television. I know it was all a dream. Now back to reality. Or did I really want a mother and father in the household and end up like my friend who father touches and sleeps with her? She has to carry that burden every morning when we walk three blocks to school. I really didn't know what life I wanted but I know I didn't want my life. I know I wanted the simple shit. The free shit that doesn't cost anything shit. Praying over and over for some type of change to occur.

Could I have a mother who is nurturing? A mother who will sit me down on three stacked pillows with the hair grease and brush by her side. Both of us engaged in conversation while she is braiding my hair and adding all the barrettes and hair bows to it. When she finishes she will add to my self-confidence by telling me how amazingly beautiful I am. I would love my hair so much just because of the bonding moment we would have. But once again it's all a dream. I have the coke head mom who puts her pointer finger in her mouth to put spit on it to whip the corner of my mouth. The mother who calls me bitches time and time again. Damn, is Bitch my nickname? Moonie became a thing of the past and Bitch was present.

Daydreaming about the pops I always would want would be regular, ideal, I mean the average fucken Joe. The father who truly admired his daughter with every breath he took. The ideal father I wanted is the one who would hold my hand in public places with the assurance of safety and overall protection. The one who was proud to have a daughter such as me. The father who would let me know of all the dusty dudes I may encounter throughout life. The ones who wasn't shit and a waste of time. But nah I stop dreaming and see the pops I got. The workaholic, ladies' man. The father who could care less as long as he was with every woman he met with all the flashy clothes and shoes. Linked and herringbone chains galore. Pops always walked around like a bag of money. But your damn kids have hand me downs. Stay grateful Moonie, stay grateful. But I just couldn't, for what. One day is all I could say, one day change will come!

Finally, the day has come pops has come to rescue us. He told us mom is getting help with her fourth child, her addiction. She was going to rehab in South Carolina. I guess she was going there because that's where her mother lived. Who knows I know I wasn't trying to figure it out because I was over figuring out adult things. So at this point, I feel like all those prayers I sent up to God he was answering them one by one. Mother aborted her fourth child and chose us instead. 14 now living in VA, I don't know how to feel. I have so many emotions going through me. Dad is what you can say is trying to turn a different leaf. This time seems sort of different more stability and less stress for me. New state, new school, and a new life. I wasn't eight anymore but she was still inside of me no matter how much I tried to get rid of her.

It is so important for us to have this new life. No one knows us at all. No one knows dad as the cheater or mother as the junkie. Yes, no one knows us here. Yes to the new life. No one knows that dad left us so many times. Spending many of his nights with different ladies. Not caring if we even ate at all. No one knows that mother had a fourth child that she loved more than her other three children. The one she craved more and more with every hit. The crazy thing is you are supposed to love all your children the same no matter what. I was still me but refreshed. School was great new people, new friends. Smiling more, laughing more, things that I normally didn't do because a frown always embraced me.

New environment but still not seeing much of dad. Different place, but same stuff I guess you could say. Yes, we had a nice place to stay and lots of food, but I still felt empty inside. Everyday life with not many complaints. Better than being with my aunt many may say. Mother was doing so much better which was such a weight off my barely 15-year-old shoulders. The fourth child vanished. Time went by and so many changes took place.

Growth was made with so many people around me. Being in high school now and knowing and learning a lot from the streets and my sister. Yes, my educators and support systems were the streets and my sister. I was taught very well I must say. I came into high school still struggling with myself but I was so determined to find her. Headstrong, outspoken and loud was what I always presented. This is me and who cares who likes it because this was my attitude. The advice dad gave to me upon entering high school is to get good grades and don't get pregnant. The grades have and will always be a breeze. The pregnant part ummmmmmmmmm.

I started dating the popular guy. When he stepped into our school, I can say he was nice looking and had on the newest stuff. He seemed calm and like he was kind of a show-off. He looked like he was worried about a lot of the wrong things. Every girl almost went for him except me. His finesse is what got me swept off my feet and his everyday persistence. He reminded me of my father in a way. How he was smiling at women all the time. Father's smile could light up a room. That is what drew these women to him I bet. I was in the same situation with Mr. Popular and his damn smile.

Mr. Popular's smile would make you feel like you are the only one that mattered even though eventually I would find out there were other women. Me and Mr. Popular got Popular really quick I must say but he was my first serious relationship. My other relationships would last weeks or a couple months you know how that goes. So many people hated our relationship while there were many that admired it. Twin day came we were dressed alike from head to toe. Where I was; he was there and vice versa. Step practice and competitions he was there. Basketball practice and games I was there. On the weekends we were a lock. Spending every day together in and out of school.

Father wasn't too happy about Mr. Popular sweeping his youngest daughter off her feet. Father let me be because of the many times he abandoned me when I was younger I guess. I guess he didn't want to ruin my happiness at all. Little did father know is that this was one of the moments I needed his guidance and comfort. I needed him to tell me my worth. I needed Father to say why was I was allowing Mr. Popular to disrespect me behind closed doors and in front of people too. I needed him to say "Why are you and her not using protection? You know better than that Moonie!" But meanwhile, father was letting me lose myself and just live the way I was going. I was allowing Mr. Popular to fuck me with no form of protection. Yes, he carried magnums but I guess that was for show and other females. I guess I should be happy that he was protecting his self when he fucked them. I allowed so much to be done to me because I was just over standing up for myself. I didn't think I was worth any more than this. Dad's little girl was all I wanted, but dad couldn't see that and if he did he just let me remain broken. Dad was blinded by all the materialistic things to keep me laced with the up and coming clothes and shoes.

All I wanted Father to do was lace me with love and time. As my relationship grew with my boyfriend, then my dad allowed him to spend the night. Yes, I was fifteen years old and we took full advantage of my dad. I spent the night at his house on school nights. His mother would take us to school in the morning. My friends thought this was the coolest thing out. They had wished they parents would let them do this. Taking advantage of Father was easy because he didn't care about me at all right now or even before. Yes, I give it to him, Father was trying a little bit. I rode with father to different places sometimes, we watched movies and we "politicked".

He started to earn a small spot in my shallow heart. Staying on track in school was successful because I did graduate and guess what I was not pregnant. I did listen to dad about a little something. Umm now what to do because I really didn't want to go straight to college. I was only 17 years old. Drinking and partying is what I chose. Let's add a little bit of smoke in there too. Everyone was going through this phase. Well, the phase is what everyone's parents were saying we were going through. What I was doing was disappointing to Pops but he still didn't own his stripes to say anything if you wanted my opinion. Yes, only seventeen under his roof but who cares.

I eventually went to a trade school and became a medical assistant but that wasn't really doing anything for me because Virginia wasn't paying much to start in a position like that. Well in the process of job searching and staying level-headed, me and Mr. Popular ended up pregnant. Yes, I was twenty and pregnant. Yes I was grown in my eyes and yes I graduated but I still was under my parents' roof. The biggest fear I had has come to pass. I was pregnant with my first child and I had to bring it to my father. I had to confront father with the face of fear and disappointment.

Silence gathered in the room. The room only had me, my father and my unborn child. My stomach was tight and bubbly. What are you going to do, father asked? My reply was to keep it. In my head, my full sentence had asshole on the end of it. He asked me how I will take care of the baby. I answered while swallowing my fears, I will find a way to take care of my baby. But what I really wanted to say to him is that you have the nerve nigga, you didn't even take care of me. But I just remained silent after the question. Father rubbed his shiny head and replied to me and said I only want what is best for you Moonie. Despite my actions in the past and I will be there for you. He hugged me which I embraced because this was the first hug I received from him. He was a man of no affection and emotion. So, I had to take whatever, he was giving.

Mr. Popular got locked up and remained in the system until our son was born. Yes I know it's sad but hey the story of my life. Son was three months when he got out of jail. And just in case you were wondering yes I was there the whole step of the way. Writing letters to the jail, visiting, phone calls, whatever to make sure he kept his head up while he was in there. During this period me and dad became closer I must say. The weird thing father had changed so much that I forgot about the many things from the past that he did, I guess you can say my shallow heart was disappearing. I no longer thought about what he did or what he could have done. The thing that mattered the most to me is the right now and the future me and father had to make our relationship better. Being pregnant with son was a stress and also finding out father had prostate cancer. This beat all of us down but being that he found out quick he had surgery and it was removed. Thank God, yes I thanked God something I was doing more often these days. I knew I went through so much during my adolescent years but I knew God wouldn't take father at a Primetime like this. He finally regained his trust and his relationship with his kids.

My son was finally born. What a day what a day. So many emotions. But father was there and sister as always. Mother was there too. Father stayed with me one night of my hospital stay. He jumped up every time I moved it was sort of amazing that we were finally on the same accord. He cared now this is everything I ever wanted from father. As the years went by me, sister and brother spent so much time with him. He comes by our separate homes and we would do things together. After his surgery, we all went to Kings Dominion on a family outing. Even experiencing his wife Mary J Blige. No this wasn't his wife but you couldn't tell him she wasn't. The concert was awesome it took my breath away. I could finally brag about my pops, I became grateful for Father's Day. Me and Mr. Popular ended up going our separate ways for many different reasons. Son was now two and I would have loved for son to have a two parent household but it wasn't meant to be. The fights, disrespect, the pain, cheating, and lying became a bit too much. He reminded me so much of what father used to be. Taking care of home but never there. Handling women but not your girlfriend. Walking around acting like you have a happy home but you live in a broken home. In order for me to continue living, I had to mend the broken pieces of me and also put me first. With father coming around a lot more he showed me how to embrace me. Mr. Popular didn't deserve the new me and my journey.

Mother and father divorce was finally final so I knew the time would come that father would find someone that deserved the new man that he had become. He will get a woman that he could tell about his past with no judgment but appreciate and thank God for the man that he has presented to her. Me and sister would always say that whoever dad ended up with that we wouldn't call her stepmother. Whoever the lady he ended up with we would chop her up and put her in a blender. No evidence left behind, ha-ha. We couldn't risk someone taking our father

that we always wanted and needed away from us. He finally
was living up to being a father. Despite our wrong thinking
dad was graced with a beautiful amazing, caring and loving
woman. She loved dad she loved don she loved all of us.
No, I'm not saying that because she brought me a Dooney
and Burke purse.

    I knew the day would arrive when dad would marry
her and move to Georgia. I accepted her as my stepmother
which I know that is shocking; damn it's shocking to me too.
He still called every day. He was there when he could be.
Long talks on the phone laughing and us hysterically being
us. So happy and free was in the sound of his voice. The
calls started to taper off some. Less calls, less old father's
voice. No more jokes, no more much of anything. My
thoughts of flashbacks started to present themselves again.
Did he abandon me for a woman? What was it? Did she
take pops away? I was so full of many emotions.

    At this point, I was overwhelmed in a state of
disbelief. The phone rings and the Caller ID displays
father's name. I picked up in a state of confusion. Hurt and
pain displayed in my voice; I say hello. He speaks in his
deep tone. Hey, Moon doggie he said. The hurt and pain
disappeared slowly. A smile slowly gathered in my face.

We talked, chopped it up a bit and the call ended. I felt bad because I damn near killed him ten times in my head over and over again. My heart couldn't bare me losing my dad over again. The calls with father weren't everyday anymore but I understand his new life with his new wife. I was happy for his new life because he was a better man. A better man; he was everything I ever wanted. Dads calls started to taper off again and I didn't have time for this again my heart couldn't handle it. So instead of waiting, I called him no answer from his cell. So being that it wasn't any answer on his cell I called the house phone.

The house phone was answered on the second ring by his wife. I said hello even though I was not feeling her at this moment because all I wanted to do was speak to my dad. I felt like she was being his gatekeeper. Why is she asking me all these questions? Why is she asking me am I ok like no I'm not I wanted to speak to my dad. Duh, this is the reason for the call. She asked so many questions and then she asked me a question that hit my heart. Did she say are you sitting down? I said yes, what is going on. She said these last couple of weeks it's been so hard for us. So hard for your father because he has been trying to figure out how to tell you all. He asked me to talk to you all, but I really don't know how to execute it. I'm on the other end of the phone like spill it. It can't be any worst then all the other times he left us with no food and other things that were more important than us. When she said my father's cancer came back it was like slow motion took over. I couldn't breathe, tears just took over me to where it felt as if I was drowning. She said he can barely talk or walk. Everything my father ever was had vanished in a matter of a couple weeks.

That last phone call, we had together was the last one. Hell no I was not going for it. Sister and brother found out as well and we went to Georgia to take a look for ourselves. The wife told us he was in the hospital due to a bed sore, but we were like all this is minor like dad got his prostate removed. It's no way in hell that this is happening. We arrived late that night and walked into to father's hospital room. He was sleep. The doctor came in because his shift was ending just to see pops before it ended. He introduced himself and that's when he uttered the words to us that father had six or fewer months to live. He exited the room and my knees became weak. My eight-year-old self-came out as my father looked lifeless as he laid on the bed. Everything was stripped from him in the blink of an eye and I couldn't do anything about it.

Things became worst for dad, I must say for all of us. Back home not getting no sleep popping up all times of night. Talking to wife all day every day now to check in on him. Dec 29, 2009, a day before my mother's birthday I received a call from sister at 3 in the morning. My heart sunk into my chest, I said hello. She didn't say anything. Ten long seconds went by and she said he is gone. I said, "What!" and she said he is gone. All I could do was yell. I yelled and it seemed like no one could hear me. The yell that you never hear. I felt like I was in a dark room that had no end. It was like I was running with no endpoint. He was gone and I couldn't even begin to believe it. His service and everything is still a washout for me. I am lost now. I have two boys who need me, but I don't know where I am. She was buried with pops on January 8, 2010. Time goes by and my life is at the bottom.

400 feet deep underwater not caring about anything. Have you ever been underwater and it felt like forever before you reached the top. You get to them and when you get from underwater you take a deep breath when you get to the surface of the water. You look and your chest is tight and your heart is beating fast. That is how I felt every second knowing he was gone. I cried like a little baby. I was twenty-four years old lost with nowhere to go. Not eating, not doing anything. As days and weeks went by I started to feel sick to my stomach throwing up and I thought it was due to me not

eating. That wasn't the reason at all. I was pregnant with my baby girl. She saved me. She saved me from my shortcomings.

Father knew while watching over me that if I was with child that I would take care of myself. I wouldn't harm myself in any type of way while carrying this baby. Still, tears fall and I have my bad days. But I see the importance of life and I see the kids, my growth, and my life. I am still missing you. I'm missing you father, your smile, your jokes, and your heart. Your baby girl carries you and still looks up to you. The man I want my boys to become or even half of what you were. The structure of a man is what I see now. The man that stood up and owned up to your mistakes. Admitting to all your wrongdoing. You may have never uttered an "I love you" to me once but I can say the joy you brought to me, the protection you embraced me with, and the courage you taught me was all the love a child could ever ask for. And for that, I would be forever grateful to even have a father like you.

The hardest day of my life was knowing I would never see your face again, hear your voice, touch your hand, and so much more. Everything I went through prepared me for losing you and I wouldn't change anything. I'm missing you and I'm missing me. I'm missing the girl I use to be the replica of you but one day I will find her again. I am learning and growing daily. But I miss the girl that left January 8, 2008. Her smile, her ambition, her overall happiness. She will present herself again soon. I will continue to miss you pops.

Missing you 10-26-1950 to 12-29-2009.

If You or Someone You Know has questions about prostate cancer, then contact, Cancer Treatment Centers of America at (855) 900-5414.

MO MONEY, MO PROBLEMS

By: Lakeesha "Klu" Atkinson

My locker was the set next to the senior lockers on the backside wall. On this day, I left my friends early to go grab my books. As I was entering my combination, 26-38-22, I felt someone standing beside me so I looked up and a male voice said, "Good morning." I look up and say "What's up, Scott?"

It was just another day. It was my freshman year at Woodrow Wilson High School and I was getting used to my daily routine. We were in the old Manor High School building so the walls were still covered with Manor Mustangs. As you walk past the office on the wall to the left were pictures of the older classes from the 80's. For a while, we were repping' two mascots, the Mustangs, and the Presidents. The carpets were covered in this rust orange color throughout.

A couple of steps through the office walkway was the cafeteria to the left. I mostly got the same thing, a sausage biscuit that was already pre-wrapped so you can grab and go and I would switch between the pineapple-orange juice (the one in the plastic container with the thick aluminum lid that you have to poke more than once with your straw to make a hole) and the small miniature carton of grape juice (take one sip and it's gone). I would always wait until I finished eating to drink my juice for those reasons.

Once you got your food, you would go to the cashier in the line and either pay or enter your student ID number, which was a 6-8 digit number for free lunch. I qualified for free lunch, so this number lived in my memory forever. I later realized that the first two digits were the year you started school. The thing to do was to get off the bus, head to breakfast, and then chill on the Square until the morning bell rung.

The Square was the hangout spot. It was just as it was called, a huge square. The 2-4 steps that lead to the top served as chairs along with the brick corners that was on each end. Everyone had their unclaimed areas on the square, meaning no one had to say this is my area, you just knew because that's where they would gather every day. It was the center of the school. From almost every wing, you were a few steps from it. If you didn't sit on the Square, then you would just stand on the outside of the lockers, in between, or on the backsides. The lockers basically outlined the square. From the center of the Square, you could see everything looking left, right, and forward except for all the senior lockers. You could see the first two rows, but the others were a peep around the corner.

I was surprised to see Scott. The last time I saw him was our 6th grade year. We were in a puppy love not serious "tell your friends to get with my friends" type of thing. Scott talked to my friend Shanette and I talked to his friend Isaac. He was much chunkier back then. Seeing him for the first time in years was a bit different. He stood about 5'10, light complexion, light brown eyes, the waist was about a 34 now. From the shape of his nose which was long and pointed, you could tell he was biracial. His father was white and his mother was black. His hair was an auburn color and his edge up was as sharp as his smile. When he smiled, his pearly white teeth would stand out between his mini red lips. "How have you been?" he said. "Cool," I said. My answers were short, but every question led to a follow-up. We ended up catching up and talking about what we did in the summer until the bell rung. "I'll talk to you later," I said. Then, I grabbed my books out of my locker and headed to class.

The next days to follow, Scott would show up at my locker in the morning and even between classes. One day I started to take notice of his daily outfits. Based on what he wore, you would have thought he was sponsored by Hanes and Nike. He would wear a fresh pair of DC's (Air Force 1's) and a shirt to match. If the DC's were burgundy, then his T-shirt was that color as well.

One day I asked, "How many pairs of DC's do you have?" Scott replied, "Just about all of them." When he talked, he smiled at the same time and chuckled in between his words. "So where do you work?" Scott responded fast without hesitation "the streets". I laughed and said, "So you sell drugs?" "Here and there." In my mind, I was left to figure out what here and there was, but at that point, it was his honesty and transparency that drew me further into him. I gave him my house phone number. We would talk every day after basketball practice like clockwork. No matter what he was doing, he was home to catch my call. If I was late from basketball practice or had an away game, my timing was off and soon as I got in the house my mom or my younger brother would say "Scott called."

The "like" for him had started and in my mind, it felt wrong. The feelings were mutual so we had a conversation. I decided to call Shanette. She moved so she was going to school in another district now. "What's up girl," Shanette said when she picked up the phone line. "Nothing much, I need to ask you something." "You remember Scott?" "Yea I remember red chunky Scott..." We both laughed. "How was the relationship? Did you have feelings for him?" Shanette said, "Nah, it wasn't even nothing like that." Then I said we have been talking for a while, but nothing serious, and I like him, but I didn't want to go further with him if it would be an issue or affect our friendship..." She said "Nah,

yall good" again and "I didn't really like him like that..." I
said "word". She said, "Yea do you Klu..." Klu was my
nickname, well it was actually Klu-Klu, but somewhere in
middle school between DJ Clue coming up in the industry,
then it was shortened.

People would say Clue Clue-like DJ Clue would
sound on a mixtape track with his voiceovers or just Clue. I
kept my spelling as Klu. After I hung up the phone with
Shanette, I felt like a weight was lifted off my shoulder. I
should have been made the phone call. I was wrong, but
everything worked out. That was the one thing that was
stopping me. I called Scott right after that and told him I
told Shanette and she was cool and you could hear a sigh of
relief in his voice. Our conversation was short that day. I
think we both were thinking, what's next?

Scott and I were finally official. Our relationship in
my mind was perfect. We didn't argue which was crazy.
Even though Scott sold drugs, I was never pressed for
money or asked him for anything. He used to always ask me
did I need anything. Besides food, the answer was usually
no. My brothers were in the streets as well, so I didn't want
for anything. I always had money. I didn't go on a school
field trip with less than $500. We lived at that time in the
white and light blue house at 2223 Portsmouth Blvd. It

wasn't a day that went by that I didn't see my brothers with money. In the evenings, whether it was in the sunroom of the house or the den, the sounds of Master P "make 'em say uhhhh" and the aroma of marijuana filled the air. I use to always just chill and observe. The sunroom was where the studio was at and my brothers and their friends would record music. From time to time, even I would get on the track. When they weren't there, I would practice my lyrics and mix songs together. Our favorite instrumental track was Onyx "Last Days". I was used to seeing my brothers bring home coke and then cook it up.

My oldest brother, Kut never really let me watch him. When he used to mix before he would cook it up, he would use his t-shirt to cover up his nose and mouth so he wouldn't breathe in the smell. Every time I came in the door, he would say "Klu get outta here". Weed was a different story. Kut would bring home black trash bags filled with weed. I would watch him bag up nickels, dimes, dubs, halves, and ounces. Nickels and dimes were bagged in jewelry plastic bags and anything greater was bagged in Ziploc bags without the smart zip. The metric table on the back of my elementary composition books was starting to make sense.

Once I learned, when my brother wasn't home, he would get people who wanted to buy to come around the back and I would ask what they want and hand them the bag. The looks on my brother's friends' faces were priceless. I didn't have a legit job at the time, but I always figured out a way to make money. You can say this started when I was 8 years old with my grandfather. I use to be afraid of him when he would come over to the house. He would knock on the door with a distinct knock of knocking in a rhythm like "dun dun da dun dun" and then saying "Beep Beep". Beep Beep was his name. By the time he said Beep Beep on the other side of the door, I was out, running down the hall and into my room. Soon as he would come to my room and talk to me, I would just yell and start screaming. He used to tell my mom something not right with the girl and ask, "Why is she scared of me?"

I still don't know why I was scared. Besides my grandmother, he was the first old person I had ever encountered. Maybe I had a phobia of senior citizens. It was one day, my grandfather came over and he needed some money because his Social Security check hadn't come yet. My mom called me in the living room. I was in my room when she yelled, "Keesha". I said "Yes". "Come here, Beep Beep want to ask you something". That was the slowest walk down the hall. I got to the living room and stood behind my mom.

My grandfather was like "Baby girl I need $20 from you until I get my check. You give me $20 and I will give you $40 back." I went to the room and got the $20 out of my silver pig shaped bank and went back to the living room and handed it to Beep Beep. He said "thank you" and put on his hat and walked out the door. Two days later, Beep Beep came back and I opened the door for him. He said, "Here you go grandbaby". It was two $20 bills. I had doubled up my money that quickly. From that day, I always wanted to be around my granddad. I even use to up my offerings and convince him to borrow money from me. "Granddad, I got $40 if you need it." $40 turned to $80. A hustler was birthed.

The little money came from selling candy and sunflower seeds. I would go to the grocery store and buy the bulk packs of candy bars and seeds. Then, figure my profit from each bag. The large amounts of money came from hustling my brother friends in video games. I had mastered NBA Live. I rarely lost a game. I could beat anybody. Then one night, my brother brought his friend over and he was saying you can't beat lil sis. His friend was like yeah right. I was like put 50 on it. So we played and I killed him.

I had won my first 50. I was like run it back for another 50. He lost again. I made 100 dollars in less than an hour. My mind was racing. I went upstairs that night and went to bed thinking if I hustle him for 100 a day, that's 500 a week. I was always calculating numbers in my head. This was no different.

The next day I came home ready. I got on the game practicing until my brothers got in around 7. His friend came in with a smile. He knew what was up, game on. I raised the stakes. Let's play for 75. In my mind, I didn't know how long this would last, so I wanted to make as much money as possible. I was victorious again. We were still playing every week. The universe works in mysterious ways. I didn't hear from Scott much. He was out in the street hard. He would call to check on me, but I always would be like, let me call you back, I'm busy. We were both chasing paper. It was one day my brother friend came in with this solid gold Cuban link chain with an iced out cross pendant.

I was a jewelry head and that was my dream necklace. He said, "What are we playing for tonight Klu?" I said, "Your chain". He laughed and looked at me like I wasn't serious, but I was. It was a tight game. It's like he had been practicing. It was like March Madness down to the buzzard. Funny, that's how I won. I stole the ball from him and ended the game with an open floor dunk. Everybody was like ohhhhhh. I rubbed my hands together as to say off with your chain. He reneged on me winning the chain, but he gave it to me and I wore it like it was mine. I had it for a couple of months.

When you are making money, it's easy to get distracted. I was missing my best friend, Scott. We were inseparable, but during this time, we both understood, but it was time to see him again. Being around him always made me smile. We would talk about any and everything. The attraction was beyond physical and more mental. I called and said, "Let's get up this weekend." That weekend, we went to Chesapeake Square. It's crazy, between the two of us, we always had a decent amount of money.

We were so tight with our money. I remember him saying "Are we walking or catching the bus?" I was not walking to Chesapeake Square even though in reality it's a straight shot down Portsmouth Blvd. I was like huh, we taking a cab? I will pay for it. He was like, "I got it." He didn't never like me to pay for anything, but today was going to be different. When we got to Chesapeake Square, I headed straight to Footlocker. He was so simple.

I already knew I was getting him some DC's and a tee to match. "Which ones you want?" I said. He said,

"You don't have to buy me shoes," I said, "I know that, but you do so much for everybody else, people should take care of you sometimes." He really couldn't debate about that. Something probably flashed in his head about all the things he did or maybe the last amount of money he gave to someone. He picked out the red and black DC's and I got him a black and red tee. I bought me a pair of Air Max 95 and we got something to eat at the food court and headed back home. He chilled at my house for a while and then when it got dark, he walked home. When he walked he would always call and say, "I was just calling to let you know I made it home safe." "Alright," I said. Then we both would in sync say "good night" and hang up the phone.

My birthday was coming up and it was only during the holidays and my birthday that I wanted things. Those days were important to me so my stubbornness went out the window. My birthday falling in December was a gift and a curse. It was mid-December, so I still expected a birthday gift, a Christmas gift, and a Valentine's Day gift. For my birthday, I wanted some Jays (Jordans). The ones I wanted were different. These were the wrestling Jordans. My favorite color was red so any shoe with red in it was a go. I didn't care how ugly it was. Scott came through and got me the shoes. He came over a day after Christmas and gave me

the box. It wasn't wrapped or anything. He wanted me
instantly to see without waiting to unwrap and going through
a gift bag.

On Valentine's Day, he called me early in the
morning and said meet me at the crib around 1. I got up
after that to get my mind right. I was going to walk. I guess
walking for us for therapy. When I walked from my house
to KP (Academy Park), I always felt at peace. It was my time
to get myself together and think about life in general and my
future plans. It was during my walks that I questioned my
sexuality and whether I wanted to be with a male or female.
Those lasted only seconds because I would replace those
thoughts back with Scott and how perfect he was. When I
got to his house, his boys were in the living room playing the
game. The aroma from the kitchen smelled good. Scott
had on an apron. In my head, I was like this dude really has
on an apron. I was laughing on the inside. He never cared
who was around. When I arrived, it was all about me.

He told me to go to his room and chill and he would
be there in 30 minutes. He quickly kicked his boys out and
said: "Yall gotta go, Keesha is here and it's Valentine's Day."
I could hear them from the room. They tried to clown him
and joke and say, 'you whipped, you whipped." When
someone said that it basically means you are gone head over

heels over your partner and they got you wrapped around their fingers. He would laugh and joke back "At least I got a girl." They finally left. I heard the door close and he walked back into the kitchen. The walls out KP were so thin that no matter how loud you had the TV, you could still hear everything that was going on.

Scott came into the room with a plate. On the plate was a steak and a potato. He had the silverware on it, the fork and one of those good cutting steak knives. He went back to the kitchen to get the A1 Sauce. He then opened up his drawer and pulled out a card and said Happy Valentine's Day's. I opened up the card and it had money in it. That was the first time anyone I was with had ever cooked for me. I devoured every bite of that steak. He didn't even fix himself anything. I wasn't even trying to share mine, but I offered him some and he said no, "Enjoy". We laid together after that and watched "Love Jones". Mid-way through the movie, we lost interest in watching and turned to each other and got lost in an intense kissing session.

When basketball season was over, he would walk to my house from KP every day and we would watch Jerry Springer or walk down to the basketball court and play against each other. The Olympic Sports Club court was a couple of blocks down on Portsmouth Blvd. When we played, I rarely won. He had a jump shot like Steve Kerr. I use to always say that's your white side. After each jump shot, he would say "cookies." That would always annoy me. "That's all you got is a jumper," I said. I would get mad and post him up and bow him really hard and score. He would just smile and get the ball and make another jump shot. That was our day when the weather was nice "Love & Basketball."

Money was still pouring in. Scott was making more money than he had when I first met him. I could tell because he was buying more stuff for his room and still buying every pair of DC's. He brought a new bed set, every possible game system, a new TV, and some wall art. He was giving his mom money for bills and also buying things for his sister. On Sunday's when the paper came to my house, I would pull out the department store weekly ads. I would eye mainly the electronics and put an imaginary circle in my mind of everything I wanted to buy. I remember looking at the Rent-A-Center Ad and seeing a TV with the VCR/DVD combo. I had to have it.

I told my mom I wanted it, and she said her favorite line ever, "How am I supposed to get it; with my good looks?" Me being smart, I use to always say "yes with your good looks". When I had something in my mind I wanted, nothing could really stop me from getting it. I was going to make it happen one way or another. I did some research on how I could get the TV myself. The ad said you can rent to own and the TV would only be $22 a week. I could definitely handle that. Looking back, I still don't understand why I didn't just buy the TV outright. I was penny-pinching and losing at the same time. Anyone knows it's easy to get a TV from Rent-A-Center, but by the time you finish paying for the TV with weekly payments, you paid for two TVs. I called over the phone and did the application. I told them I was 18. Even back then, they didn't check your ID.

After I made the call, the TV was delivered the next day. The Rent-A-Center people knocked on the door and my mom answered. They said delivery for Lakeesha Atkinson. I already knew it was the TV. My mom was like "did you order a TV?" I was like yes. She was looking surprised and mad at the same time. You weren't going to fuss me out in front of the furniture guy. She figured as long as it's not in my name. I signed my contract and took the TV upstairs to my room. My mom said, "As long as you make your own payments". I ended up opening up an account with Fingerhut and ordering some jewelry out of their catalog. Scott would always say "Did you ask your mom?" She is going to fuss you out." I didn't care. It was my money.

Through the smiles, there was something inside that caused Scott to worry a lot. I could tell by looking in his eyes when it was just us. Through the back of my house, once you got on the deck, it was another area where concrete was laid behind the shed. Then through that area of the yard was another fenced in part where you could go to the left or walk straight through. It was just some additional land of grass, however, when you walk all the way through, it leads to Charles Peete Baseball Field. We would go sit on the benches of Charles Peete field and just talk.

I would ask Scott what was on his mind and he would always reply, "Life!" "What do you mean life?" I said. "I just feel uneasy at times" "I don't know what it is, I feel like no matter what I do, somebody is always waiting and watching." "Maybe you should stop selling drugs," I said. "Then how am I going to take care of my family," Scott replied. "Get a regular job," I mumbled sarcastically. "I am, it's just not the right time." Scott would always say that when I would say that to him. In my mind, he really didn't have a choice. He was a family man and other then God family was first. He carried so much on his plate being the man of the house along with not having his father around.

When I would ask him about reaching out to his dad. He would say, he doesn't deal with "niggas." That added to his pain that he held inside. He had resentment towards him because the thought of any way abandoning their child was cruel. He took great pride in being a good father in the future whenever he had kids. It was always something in the back of his mind of either dying, going to jail, someone setting him up, or absent dad dysfunction. I guess his gut feeling was right.

Eventually, when you're hustling in the streets, it will catch up with you. Something is going to happen. One of my classes I signed up for was JROTC (Junior Reserve Officers' Training Corps). The class basically prepared you mentally if you had any plans of joining the military. Our JROTC was Army based. Before class each day, we had to first learn the creed and recite it every day. For some reason on the "I do not lie, cheat, or steal, and will always be accountable for my actions and deeds" part, the class used to get loud and everybody would glimpse at each other with a side eye.

The JROTC ball was coming up. It was going to be my first time dressing up in a gown and wearing heels. It's like the more money you make, the more problems you have. I was a tomboy. I didn't like dressing up. My everyday wear was a t-shirt, sneakers with jeans or shorts. I wore my hair either in braids or a ponytail. I told Scott and he was excited about going. Now, who's hot, who not? He was like "I'm going to pay for everything, your dress, shoes, hair, my tux, and the limo." The limo??? Yea we going in style. I want this night to be beautiful and I will do anything to make that happen. I told him, just worry about you and the limo and I got my stuff. He said "You so stubborn."

"Bruise too much, I lose too much". I picked up the phone. "I just got robbed." It was one week away from the JROTC ball. "They took everything, my money, my game system and my leftover rock..." I didn't even ask was he ok? All I cared about was him taking care of his part for the Ball. "Are you serious?" Yes, I gotta figure out something, Scott said. I was so pissed, I said: "Yes figure out something and don't call me back until you do." I hung up on him. That was probably the first time I hung up on him. He called right back and I said: "I don't want to talk to you right now." At that point, it was in my head that I was going by myself. All I could say in my head is "this nigga." I told him to stop selling drugs.

I gave him the cold shoulder in school and didn't talk to him much. It's like nothing bothered him. He still said good morning and have a good day. "Yo, I thought I told you that we won't stop". Scott came to my house. I stood at the door and he said I just wanted to let you know everything will be ok. It was 2 days until the Ball. He showed me a crack rock the size of a tennis ball, which hadn't been cut yet. After that, he left and said I'm going to be out all night and I may not come to school. I didn't ask any questions. It probably was consignment.

The day of the Ball, I got a call that morning from Scott saying I'll be there to pick you up at 5. Me still in doubt, said "ok". I went to the hair shop in Tower Mall early. I was in there all day. It was the first time I cut my hair. I trimmed off and curled the top and left it long in the back flipped. When I got home, I must have looked good, my little brother said "my sister is beautiful" My mom was even smiling. It was about 4:15 pm. I went upstairs to get dressed. My dress was given to me by Godmother. It was cream, sleeveless with the back out and on the straps were pearls. I heard my mom yell "Scott here" from upstairs.

I went to look out my mother's room window and it was a black limousine outside. I smiled so hard, but I had to get myself together before I went downstairs. I knew Scott would have this infamous grin on his face. I was right. I walked downstairs and everybody was waiting. I looked up and he was smiling and looking fine as ever in his cream tux. His whole get-up was crème de le crème. Crème down to the socks. He didn't say anything. We took pictures and then we got in the limo. I lose my touch, never that. I looked at him and at this point, he was all teeth. He was probably holding back because my brothers were grilling him.

It wasn't a "first time meeting you grill", but more so of we know what goes down after balls and prom look. "Damn baby, you look good." He just kept staring. "Didn't I tell you everything was going to be ok?" I was nodding to all his questions. I was somewhere else with sexual thoughts on the brain. He really made it happen. He just kept tapping his foot. I went over to him and laid in his lap and looked into his eyes and said: "I love you..." He said, "I love you more and until the death of me." I smiled and said, "Tonight will be beautiful. I'm going to make it up to you. I will never doubt you again as long as we are together."
In memory of Scott "Eugene" Upshur. Rest in Paradise

*If You or Someone You Know has questions about grief, then contact, https://grief.com/group-resources/ *

NASTY BOY

By: Ashley Starling

"Nasty boy, you nasty! Nasty boy, you nasty! Nasty boy, you nasty!" How many times have we said we looking for a nasty boy? Someone who dresses their tail off with that mmmhmmm smell good cologne, dressed nicely with matching swagger? Not only do they dress and smell good but they can also fulfill your every desire when they pull that G string down south? Oww! I think it's safe to say it almost every girl's dream to find that nasty boy whether in a relationship, casual, or even married couples. My last ex was definitely a nasty boy. The attraction was off the chain and the chemistry was fire. We moved so fast because it just flowed like that. The night we met up, it was just on and popping. I got to hit the shower with the shavers/trimmers, razors and hit all the areas to get ready for a great experience. You gotta make sure to get the yoni right.

Anyways, I greeted him at my door with a come in and he welcomed me back with a nice juicy kiss. The tongues were clicking and clacking. He picked me up and carried me to the bedroom and I fell right into lust. He took care of my body and I took care of his. There was no holding back, no hesitation, no thinking or stopping for breath for a few hours. The pleasure stemming from that session had my eyes crossing. Let's be honest, how many times have we just said: "Maannn, somebody going to get it today..." We fantasize about what's going to happen even daydreaming about it leading up to the moment. Started rubbing all over my body in the shower and end up getting off a nut before the session started. This is not for the virgin ears or eyes. I/We are born to be desired so it's only right that we are taken care of in EVERY way imaginable.

In addition, to men wanting their every desire fulfilled, I want the same. As much as I want it for myself, I want you to be desired as well. But I shall forewarn you though, as much as we like to get down, there are negative looks from society and maybe your friends and family may come down on you. Your happiness may come at a pretty price if you allow it. You know those negative terms whore and sluts come into the mindset of ones thinking. The same relationship that started hot, heavy, locked and loaded with pleasure started to turn into a negative outlook that had a lasting impression. Let me explain........

To be a nasty boy is just to be a nasty boy but to be nasty girls, you get looked at like sluts and whores. How many of you have been called sluts and whores? I have heard people speak on someone else's experiences and while it might not be right in their eyes, It's not our place especially with consenting adults. We live in a society where it's okay for nasty boys to just do how they want with us and move on to the next....I mean "sex is all I can expect" right. Let me tell you that it is not right! Dudes get dapped up and praised for smashing this chic and that one like it's nothing. But contrary, if females do it then you ain't nothing but a...hoooooooeee.

In some cases, those words will follow you even throughout your relationships. I know the feeling all too well. Being single and doing me and BOOM! End up in a relationship (the situation referenced above) and he discovered that in my single days, I had occasions of getting down and having fun. Now come to find out he has been a nasty boy as well (dirty laundry I won't broadcast). I could even tell in the bedroom that he was experienced because he did some thangs to me. He had to learn somehow though, through practice, right? There were times in the relationship where past casual situationships were brought up and he looked at me with disgust in his eyes. Not only did he look at me with disgust in his eyes, he also brought it up in every argument.

He found a text message from a situationship that was over before we became a couple and I didn't respond to it. However, he said that I was still messing with this guy and how I'm a whore and slut. Every single time an argument occurred he would say go on ahead and be a whore again.

Another line he would say was "that's all you would ever be". The funny thing was I never brought up his past and what he did. Despite the past, you stick with them because of no judgment. Some men say they don't want a woman with a past but they want them to be a top-notch freak nasty borderline porn star with them.

Life is a learning experience. During the baby/toddler stages, it's self-exploration. Learning to be comfortable, familiar and confident in yourself. Why is it that some guys get jealous, controlling and insecure when they discover things about the past? DOUBLE STANDARDS!! I completely understand how females should act like a lady in business in public however once those doors closed, it's called private time for a reason. If you decide to settle down and be with one, it may or may not be issues in your relationship. Decisions will need to be made if your man starts tripping. A decision had to be made and I refused for someone or anyone to belittle and talk down to me.

If you love this person and want to make it work then you can always communicate first and figure out the issues. Sometimes just communicating in depth will smooth things over. However, it needs to be stated that the past cannot be brought up again. An unfortunate scenario, you may have to just chuck the deuces which I have tried several times and he responds by saying it's because I want to be a whore again so I wouldn't leave because I didn't want to be labeled as such. Smh. Then, I realized that nobody defines me but me. Find a man who is secure in himself, confident and secure in him choosing you. I felt like he should have been okay with my past considering everybody has one. Those are important factors that could make or break it.

More importantly, make sure he has those good nasty boy qualities that are not afraid to use them. Unfortunately, in my situation, he had the good nasty qualities to the point of breaking down the bed (yes that actually happened) but he would always assume I was cheating or just wanted to hump every man I came into contact with. Something that started so sweet ended so sourly. With that being said, that type of relationship may not be for you so.....

If you are not in a relationship and just doing you...how do you like it to be done? Do you have that one nasty boy that can do all that your fantasy requires? What is it about that one that just makes you shiver and quiver all over? The one who calls you up, say get ready and immediately jump up. May have crust in your eyes, waking up from a good nap with slob sliding down your mouth but when your nasty boy call or text, it's time to get up. The one who you ready to just give it to without hesitation because he makes them juices trickle down just from thinking about him!! Every time I thought about this man, he just sent chills through my body and to my yoni. But it was just more to it than that. He was cool and laid back. It was no pressure, no judgment just chill. Does he get you wet by sending you secret pics? I was hesitant because of the trigger (you will read later on in chapter) Do you make videos for your eyes only? For those on the more adventurous side, do you go out in public spaces and go for it? He calls you up and says meet me outside, jumps in the car and gets it in there? Yes! Yes! Yes! To all of the above.

Nothing like getting a random call to come over and do it outside in the backyard. It's pretty fun and quite the adrenaline rush. You may be thinking of ideas but be on the cautious side and always pay attention to your surroundings. Don't want to have an indecent exposure charge on your record. You doing the casual thing with no ties but it seems as if one isn't enough, do you have several for a variety of areas? You may have that one that can only satisfy you orally, so you just need to add a little more spice to your life. You may have that one that can just do it good in the bed only. Do you have that one that when you see, you already know what time it is? Relationship thing not working but needs have to be met. Don't have time to deal with all the headaches, drama and emotions of it. It's okay. Find you a good one and keep it moving.

I am a single mom who works too hard, taking care of the kids, working all day and night, stressed out, need to vent, need a vacation etc., we want to be taken for a ride in our mind and let go without a care in a world. Don't be ashamed, it's your body and please it how you see fit. Always remember to be safe! If you don't want babies from your extracurricular activities then plan ahead and be prepared. Just make sure to schedule check-ups and make sure she keeps purrrrring (good discharge) down there. BTW, I've read that vaginal steams (yoni steams) are a great healthy option, along with taking herbs (be careful, they will make you fertile). I'm sure we have had several casual things once or twice, three, four or more. I'm not judging you, that's not our purpose in life! Nobody has to know what goes on behind the scenes.

Whether you choose to be open about your experiences or keep it private, just don't let people make you feel bad for choosing what makes you happy. There was one time and still maybe a smidge, that I worry about what people are saying or will be saying after reading this chapter but I have to realize that it's life and MINE!

Now I'm sure after reading the last part, you're thinking OMG! Or.....you could be like well what about married folk?? We like to be nasty boys and girls to each other. I know that's right! Shout out to the married folks who keep things spicy, hot and flaming. Applause goes out to those who try to extend/expand their marriage by yeeaarrss. This is no marriage advice whatsoever and you can do what works best for your marriage. I would just like to spark attention for those who do like them nasty boys in their union. So how do you like to give it to one another? Since you are married, do you go as far as you want to in your fantasies? Whips, floggers, handcuffs, plugs, clamps...etc.? Don't be bashful or shy. This is your life partner whom you decided to spend the rest of your life with.

It's understandable if you weren't married but you are! Ok, so maybe not as far as the whips and chains, you don't have to use those. But do you use toys? Do you sneak in the laundry room because the kids are in the way sometimes and you just need some nasty boy (husband)/nasty girl (wife) time? Done this before with ex-boyfriend, FYI! Do you get that feeling while cooking some chicken nuggets or fish sticks and just run off somewhere they can't find you? What about as simple as lighting the candles, running a bath with essential oils, massages and then getting it on for as long as you can? Whatever you decide to do, you can do to each other, and it's YOUR marriage. Get creative!

We all want a nasty boy but be careful about these nasty boys who just don't give a damn. You know the ones I'm talking about. The triple S's which stand for Self, Satisfying and Selfish nasty boys! They're not a good look whether in a relationship, casual, married etc. It's NOT A GOOD LOOK! You will be denied your rights, soul, and more messing around with them! Run fast! Run fast! Don't look back, STOP! Do not collect $200 and throw the nut back. A warning has been giving! Watch out for those who get theirs first and leave you hanging for dear life to get your own because they do not care. Make sure to add them to the do not call list. Of course, things happen but just watch the signs. It just makes me mad, like STOMP your feet mad!!

The mood is set, you been thinking about it all day and BOOM! He selfish with it! If he cannot take you to a climax high just throw the whole man away!! It's levels to it and can't get past the first because he done clocked out and left! Fire him! Yearssss ago, I dated somebody who only cared about *nuttin* for himself. He licked me like twice, pinched a nipple, bam bam and done. WTF!! When it comes to sex, it has to be a two-way open street regardless of the situation between the two. If he is unwilling to communicate, listen, and take action to your needs, then leave it alone. Nasty boys mixed with fuck boy syndrome does not end well. Ladies, I'm coming for you next! Don't just receive ALL the pleasure, you have to be willing to give as well. Listen to what he wants and how he wants it done. I'm not saying I'm the greatest, however, I do listen to how my partner wants it done and what he likes that turns him on and what he doesn't like. When he speaks, I listen and put into action but if you have multiple, you going to have to pay extra attention and concentrate to not confuse it up...

The greatest gift you can give yourself is by being a pleaser to the one you with at that moment. That is my thing and who I am as a person. I am a pleaser and love to give. The more pleasing the more they are willing to return unless it's a nasty fuck boy then you out of luck. If you have been through this, what did you do? Did you curse them out? Throw them out without their clothes on? I'm just curious to hear your experiences. For me, I just cut them completely off. Try to go as far as reading someone. How do they talk and carry themselves? If it sounds and acts like a fuck boy (and that's not your thing), please take a lesson and move on.

I've talked about several different types of nasty boys in a variety of situations because there are different definitions of what a nasty boy is. Some of them are not all good and some of them are not all bad, it just depends on the character of the person. I want to get a little deeper into the definition of a nasty boy and give you a warning about another type. A nasty boy who has no right to take away from you. Remember in this game, you always have a choice and if you not feeling it then you just aren't feeling it. We live in a risky world and some will try to take it away from you whether you consent (through manipulation) or not. I'm not sure if you would even consider this type of person a nasty boy but is a literal definition of it in my eyes. Up to this point hopefully, you have been glued in and vibing with me but I really want you to pay attention to this.

There may be a time or not (hopefully not) that you encounter a nasty boy who completely loses it and takes his frustrations out on you in a sexual way because of insecurity or something just goes off in their head and they will take your goods without your consent. Be careful, this is rape! Watch out for signs that he is angered, blamed you for something or suddenly just lashes out at you and then tries to make it up by having sex. It's time to get more personal now.

Let's talk one on one. I was in a relationship for 3yrs and the first year everything was great, it was kinda surreal. Somebody to love me, cook for me, do whatever they could for me. The bedroom had no coldness and satisfaction guaranteed on both sides. Unfortunately, circumstances change such as losing a job and a car. Accompany losing that with having the feeling of not being adequate enough and having your girl be "the man" per say. Everything seemed good on the outside, he was still making a way and spoiling me but there were also faint signs that started to come into play. Each time a disappointment came, a sign popped up. It was the tone of his voice, how quickly his temper flared or how he became meaner in flash. My first taste of it was when I just needed time to think and decided to walk the seawall.

He had called me up and I didn't feel like talking but I answered it anyway. He was like why don't you come to see me and I'm just like I just need time to unwind and relax by myself. He assumed I was with somebody and wasn't. He got upset and was like watch you going to learn. I hung up the phone and was like whatever. Later on that night, I started receiving text messages from different people asking how much would it be to see my feet and for service.....I'm like what the hell and you got the wrong number. The text kept coming in and phone calls. One guy text, I saw your ad and want to rub your feet. So I looked up the ad he was referencing and saw my picture posted on Blackplanet. It didn't show my face but it showed me in boy shorts and bare feet. My number was listed and said to contact me for pricing. I was f**king heated. I called my ex and blew his ear out.

Following that, the days of spoiling and treating on a regular basis became a way to make up for wrongdoing. The days of being loving were replaced with a way to show remorse and holidays. For Valentine's Day, he went all out. A room (where we worked at), a room full of roses, candles, big teddy bear, candies, wine, and FOOD!! Come to find out it was more beneficial to him to show off, so he could impress other girls and use that to his advantage. Later in the relationship, I just didn't feel like doing it but when you in love with someone, the sex is supposed to be a connection but now it became more of a job or habit.

In my case, it was just to get it over with. It all starts there before the unthinkable gets there. I noticed changes within myself before it even got physical. As days/months go past, I became a bubble and isolated. Depression kicked in and I wanted to disappear. It was like a sad ritual every day.

At work, I would just hide the hurt and try to put on a smile because I thought I was the problem. As much as it was killing my body and heart, I was still trying to fight. Losing faith in how I was feeling as a woman. Self-esteem running low and not caring about how I looked. Keeping quiet about what was going on at home because "what happens at home stays at home".

Nobody knew what I was going through but my momma kinda suspected but not much was said. I wasn't walking around with black eyes, broken bones, scars and bruises, it wasn't that deep yet. Usually, that's how it works. He used manipulation to break me down and cause myself to think I'm crazy. To be stripped away to make me bow down and completely be reliant and dependent on him even though I was the one hustling and bustling. And it was easy to do so because of all the loving things he did.

He paraded me in front of his family. His mom and I worked at the same job and we just looked out for one another. Who doesn't want to get in with a person's mother and family it makes you feel included? So as the good gestures and deeds turned into sorry and broken promises, I became further broke down. The days looked all the same and it was like bleak, dry, dull and just existing. Y'all ever felt that? Despite all the nasty things they would do, it just didn't matter? Not that it matters in this situation. Mental breakdown after the next. There were days I would just lie in bed and cry or I would become so angry and standoffish to others.

Entrapment was next on his agenda and to the point where I made the decisions on my own to not go out or hesitant about who I was talking to. I was scared to look at men or hell even glance at a women or exchange friendly conversation. There were days I was being questioned about who I was talking to or going out to visit. All of the questionings was because he was out being a nasty boy to other women. Those women got that dick and tried to come after me, knowing we were together. One of them came home from jail from doing a bid for him.

She stayed where I worked at and she would give me nasty dirty looks or try to be all up on him. Now, he would deny her in my face but behind the scenes, he was fucking her for stuff she brought him. On top of that, come to find out he picked her up in my car. Of course, at the time I didn't know, suspected maybe but I was in my own hell world to even pay attention. Once the truth came, the breakdowns followed after. More like feeling stupid and used. He was using me to get what he wanted and using other females as well. The nerve!

Secretly going out and being nasty with other woman but tearing me down with his disrespectful ways. Tired of being with someone who lies and disrespects me. Tired of being next to someone who had a double face. Nice and sweet on the outside but bitter, cold and mean on the inside. What happened to the person who use to care for me? So why not just leave then...... Those days were long gone out the window and if I had any chance of survival to get my life back it had to be soon or else......

The or else became very clear and very soon. I became pregnant with my 2nd child. We were having a daughter. That was a dreadful heavy burden. Afraid to tell my momma and what she would say. I was/am definitely blessed just at the time, it was like what else...?? Should have been more careful but I love my little tink pooh to the moon and back and wouldn't have it any other way. Sometimes a blessing comes after darkness. With all the breakdowns here comes the pregnancy hormones to add to it. Again on the surface being treated like a queen but on inside it was just becoming too much. I think he may have realized how much it was for him as well because one day I ended up being choked against the wall. I don't even remember why and it doesn't even matter. At that moment, it was life or death.

I started to reflect back on my life, my son, and unborn child and did not fight back. I stared into his eyes and I saw the devil, a monster, and his true character showing out. How could you put your hands on the one you claim to love and adore? The only person you said you were meant to be with? How could you choke the woman who is carrying your child? He eventually let go and I could remember doing is falling on the floor and crying. He tried to console me, apologize and say the most used up line in history......" it would never happen again".

After some time to myself, I believed that he could change or wanted to change the situation. I wanted to believe that it was just a bad dream and we could go back I just knew it. We talked things through and felt firm in my stand and told him that it will be the last time he did that. With sorrow and regret, he agreed. He said he doesn't know what happened, he just blacked out and apologized. Everything was going well from that point on but I made myself more aware of signs but I also start to come up with a plan b (It was too late for the Plan B pill).

Throughout my pregnancy, my sex drive wasn't all that high and plus I didn't even want to do to who I was with. Laying down in the bed tired from working a 12-hour shift, I just wanted to relax and chill. Next thing you know. I feel his hand trying to turn me over and I said no, I'm tired. He said lately you haven't been wanting to do anything and I said no.

That pissed him off and said you going to give it to me, just lay there and I said no. I pushed my legs together and tried to roll back over but he turned me over and got on top of me and forced himself inside of me. I was pushing and fighting him off of me. The words that came to his mouth might have been sexy at this moment but it at this moment or stage of relationship it wasn't. He said "you are mine" and "I'm never letting you go". If those words ain't scare the crap outta me! Usually, you feel good about hearing those words and be like yaasss...I'm his!! NOPE! NADA!! After he finished, I just laid there in shock like what the hell is going on.

From that point on, I just started to shut down from him even more. I didn't think I can go any lower but I did. Time speeds up and I give birth to my baby girl. She was my new found happiness, her well-being, my son well-being and my well-being depended on it. Inspiration started to fill my head. Wanting to do something to create change on the outside even I felt or didn't have the strength to do it in my own personal world. One day I was on Facebook and saw a posting about working with kids. Decided to look into it, I felt maybe I wasn't qualified for the position but decided to try anyway. So I sent a message to the director and got it! Working with little and middle school girls, I was happy. Learning to create plans, sitting on a board of an organization was new to me but it was a learning experience. The feeling it gave was indescribable because I felt like I was actually doing something that mattered. Feeling like I was breaking some type of hold on me.

A date was set to meet and greet some parents and kids for sign-ups at a football field. It was the very first sign-up date and I was preparing and getting my packets together and all my info. My daughter and I head to the field and start talking to some parents to get them interested and signed up. My cell phone starts ringing and it's him saying "bring my child back, right now". Mind you I told him where I was going and that I would be out signing up kids for the program. I said, "What do you mean I'm in the middle of talking to kids and parents?" He said I don't want my baby there and I will come to the field to get her and cause a big scene.

So I rush off home to drop her off like a big dummy and he comes out the door to get her. I have the car still running and driver door open because I plan on going back to the field. He grabs her, walks to the car, turn it off and takes the keys and puts them in his pocket. I'm arguing with him outside like "what are you doing" and he's like I don't want my baby out there mixed up in that stuff and yada yada. He then walks into the house, closed the door and locked it with me standing outside. Wow! So he really just going to do that and my name is on the lease!!

I worked hard to get that apartment not for him but for me and kids and you going to do some dumb stuff like that. I was livid and should have called the police and had him put out. That would have solved everything then because what was his purpose in my life at that point? What did he do to make a difference in my life? Instead, he was trying to pull me down in the gutter with him because that's all he felt he was. Whatever his actions were, it was a reflection of how he felt about himself. Soooo, after all that, did I put him out? Nope! Did I tell my mom? Nope! I kept it hush-hush again. Nobody needs to know my business. As much as he tried to take from me, I found a way to fight back in my own way and terms. Did I let him stop me from trying to do great things with the kids? Nope. I continued on because it wasn't about me.

The night before the meeting with parents and kids, I was sitting down, chilling and watching TV. He comes out of the blue and asks me for my phone. I said, "For what"? And he was like because I want to go through it. First off, you don't even pay for this phone! It's my property, my business and we not even married, smh barely in a relationship because mentally and emotionally I had already left. I said no. He eventually gets the phone out my hand and I start reaching for it back. He asked for my password to open the phone and I wouldn't give it to him.

He calls his mom on his phone and telling her how he has my phone etc. and I'm yelling in the background so his mom can tell him to give it back. She not even helping or saying anything but thinks I'm crazy the one. Ha! She raised a monster child. Co-signing everything he does and even lying for him. So we still arguing and going back and forth and I just said forget it and laid down and went to sleep. It quickly begins the next early morning, the day of meeting with parents. He kept asking me for my password. I got up from out my bed and went into the living room to lay down and he followed me in there. He said, "If you give me head, I will give you phone back".....I couldn't do it. Then he grabbed me to the floor and said: "Nobody can have you but me, you mine". And he was trying to force himself on me.

Pushing him off and trying to close my legs. I laid there and cried because it was happening again and I felt powerless. After he finished, I sat in the corner of my old apartment and cried. After a while, he started the shower and told me to get into it. I was in the shower balling too. How could this have happened to me? Why did it happen to me? All these questions started ringing off in my head. Later that day after being given a rape examination (humiliated) and having to track down my child because he took her....guess what I did?? Went to the field for the coaches meeting. I had told my Bestie who was one of my coaches to go ahead earlier. I made it to the field, but I was told to take it easy and maybe to rest but I wanted to stay. I didn't want to think about it. Surely though, I would be thinking about it for the rest of my life! I'm sure you are thinking why the heck you told us this story and go into depth. I wanna hear all the freaky stuff.

When you were first reading nasty boy it caught your attention and that's what I wanted to do. Pay attention! There are many definitions of nasty boys. Nasty boys can be fun and satisfying but there are other extremes of nasty boys to watch out for. The 3s' you can even say boy bye too but this is a dangerous nasty boy that I don't want any of you to encounter. The most traumatic experience of all time that will leave scars forever. I have issues with sending pictures to people of any kind. I have a bad habit of hanging on to my phone because he took mine for manipulation or just trusting someone. Also, I learned that even though I fell to my lowest, I gained strength and finally fought back.

Healing will be a battle, a will battle in your mind back and forth. I questioned my whole existence in life when being probed, swabbed and photographed during the rape exam. Questioned if I am going to make it to court physically and mentally. Questioned whether I was going to survive and be able to tell my story because people out here are upset that I locked him up. Constantly going back and forth about whether I want my daughter to visit the other side of the family.

The most painful is watching her growing up without having her father. Please heed my word and have fun playing out your fantasies with your nasty boys but please look for the warning signs! Protect yourselves in any situation and don't be afraid to stand your ground! This is a nasty boy that will never go away and I have to live with for all of my days!

If You or Someone You Know has been raped, then contact, The National Sexual Assault Hotline at 1-800-656-4673

SOMEBODY'S GOTTA DIE

By: Leatha Ballard

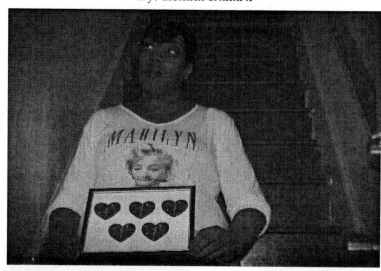

I hate you, and I don't even like that word, but you I hate. I hate your body, you're fat, you're out of shape, and you will never be anything. Look around you, everyone is popular but you. You're awkward and shaped funny. No matter what you do in life, you will be the same ugly girl. These were the thoughts of a 12-year old that was very confused.

No words could change her mind, she couldn't find a release from the thoughts that tortured her day and night. You would think the life that she lived she would keep a smile on her face. She was enrolled in one of the best private schools in VA. Her father had his own business, and her mother was a great mom that showed she loved her only daughter every day. However, no matter how good her life looked on paper, she lived in darkness. Even though she attended a Private (Christian) school, the kids were heathens. They called her names as she walked down the narrow hallways every day. "Brillo", "Hey Brillo" due to the size of her full lips. Every day while leaving school tears would form in the girl's chinky eyes.

One of her classmates one day gave her a keychain, she was so happy to get this gift from her friend. "She likes me," the girl thought. She couldn't wait for her mom to pick up her from school to show her the gift her friend had given her. "Look mom!" she showed the red keychain to her mother. Her mom yelled and said, "Where did you get this?" "From my friend she whispered" the girl knew something was wrong with the way her mom's face had turned red as a beet. "This is a keychain from a strip club," her mom said. The girl took the keychain and read it "Go-Go" she spoke out loud. Her mom had to explain to her what a GO-GO bar was. The girl was heartbroken. Her friend couldn't have known what she gave her. She went to school the next day and asked the girl about the keychain. The girl smirked and said "yeah dummy, it's a strip club" They had made a bet that the girl wouldn't know and they were right. They all stood around and laughed at her, as she stood in the middle of the hall and cried.

This was a hard lesson the girl had to learn, that people do intentionally hurt you. The girl began to contemplate suicide daily, wishing when she walked out the door someone would kill her, hit her with a car anything to end the misery she called life. Her wish never came true. "What the hell I live in a neighborhood full of violence and it seems to just pass me by," she thought to herself. One day one her classmates sent a note around the class about how ugly she was and that sealed the deal that she was going to end it all. The teacher found the note and instead of being a protector he joined in with the classmates and started to pick on the girl.

The girl couldn't believe her eyes or ears when Mr. H humiliated her. When the girl arrived home from school, she went into the kitchen and pulled the sharpest knife from the drawer and tried to slit her wrist but she didn't have the guts to do it. She then went to her father's drawer and found his gun that he thought she didn't know about it and placed it to the temple of her head. She didn't have the guts to pull the trigger. She remembered some pain pills her mom had so she went into the bedroom and found those. "How many would do the job?" she thought to herself. She took the whole bottle.

After taking the pills she felt woozy and could feel life as she knew it slipping away. She ran into the bathroom and looked into the mirror, her face was distorted like something from some special effects in a movie and she was dying. Her heart started beating slower and slower. No one was home with her, no one could help. She mustered enough strength to hold on to the sink and look into the mirror. With her strength slipping away she was able to mumble these words into the mirror, "God, don't let me die" After what seemed like an eternity she opened her eyes to find herself in her bed with her mother standing over her.

She squinted and looked at her mom. "Mommy" "yes it's me," her mom said. "Are you ok? I found you on the bathroom floor and put some water on your face." The girl just cried. Her mother held her close and prayed with her. She never told her mom of the attempt she made on her life or the thoughts she still had to kill herself even after God had saved her. This was the first attempt on my life but definitely not the last. What to do when you're going through life dealing with secrets, hiding truths that could tear a family down.

How do you smile at night when someone you trust creeps in your bedroom at night to take your innocence? Even when you speak up, nothing is done. Well, you live just as normal as you can. You see your mom smile and you don't want her to start frowning again so you keep your mouth shut. You remember the days you went to bed hungry or eating just a banana and mayonnaise sandwich. Now your freezer is full and the fridge has multiple options. You remember those days you would see your mother cry because she couldn't get food stamps and when the church couldn't/wouldn't help. So even when your heart hurts you smile. You find your own way to get through and over things without upsetting things.

You find love in others, it doesn't matter if the others are wrong for you. You just need to feel loved, so you search for love by any means necessary. The search of this "love" started in first grade with a boy named Orion, he liked you and you craved the attention. So while the teacher had her back turned to the class you let Orion rub your butt, and feel your legs. It didn't feel right but you let him do it anyway. It wasn't just attention to me it was a form of love. Something that made me feel powerful made me feel wanted. Older men had touched me before and no one knew, I didn't want to get anyone in trouble. I felt like no one would understand. I was told to keep my mouth shut and just lay there. So that's what I did. Now I wish I would have fought back, but how could I?

Here I was this skinny, little, pigtails wearing five year old. How was I supposed to fight off an adult? I would wake up and go play outside. My mom thought I was just riding my bike down the street. I would stand in the window and show the white boy my private if he showed me his. All while my mother slept peacefully in the next building. I was messed up in the head and I thought all of this was what I needed to do to be accepted. One of my molesters would say to me. "Guys like it when you're obedient" I recited this bull shit over and over in my head. I came to the conclusion if I did what the guys wanted, then it would make them like me.

This mentality followed me throughout my life. If I gave in, they would like me. Yes, I wanted love, but no I didn't think I was worthy because every time I thought I found the one, he turned out to be a disaster. Take, for instance, well let's call him Bear. Bear was who I thought was the love of my life. I met him with my Bestie when I was 18, he was the typical hood boy. Tats on his arms and legs, a drug dealer that could dress and smelled of my favorite cologne, Issey Miyake. I should have paid attention to the signs. Like when we were about to have sex for the first time, he was ready to hump me right in his sister's bed and I was dumb enough to let him.

Here he was a grown man that didn't have his own place to sex me down in; instead his sister's bed with her purple comforter and white sheets. His thing-thing wouldn't stay hard. He offered to go down on me, but I was ready to go. I lied and said I was coming on my period so he would get off of me. He gave me a sweet kiss on my forehead and walked me to the door. I felt like a million bucks. I don't know what it was but he turned me on, even though he didn't have it all together I wanted to explore a relationship with him. The turn on, turned down very quickly. I was waiting to hear from Bear but never did. Not because he wasn't interested but because he was locked up. The feds had been watching him and on one sunny day, they ambushed his cousin's crib having his family lay face down on the ground with guns to their heads. Bear was outside hiding more drugs behind the house. They were watching him for a while and he was careless so it was bound to happen. I wouldn't hear or see from Bear until many years later.

We were both guests at a mutual friend's wedding. I just knew Bear was different. That the years being locked away had changed his mentality. Due to him being older than me I figured he would want to be loyal. He didn't change his actions, he reminded me of a previous hood nigga I was with when I was 16 years old. Let's call him T Gangsta. T gangsta was true to his name in every sense of the word. He didn't take any shit from anyone. He was tall, dark and handsome. He had a raspy voice that I found sexy as hell. He was and still is a very hot-headed Alpha male. He grew up as the little kid that did no wrong, the one where his grandma thought every act of foolishness was cute. You better not try and discipline him, because she would cuss you out.

What people fail to realize is that those children grow into adults with even worse issues. I met T Gangsta through my cousin when I was a young dumb 15 year old. He was the first real "boyfriend" I had. What can I say his toughness turned me on. I was this naive, church dress wearing girl. I felt as he could protect me from the cold world. The world I feared for far too long. We would meet at the mall so he could pass me money to hold for him I was really trying hard to be his gangsta bitch. I wanted to fit the lyrics of a Lil Kim song in his eyes. All the while still going to school and not missing a day out of church. My parents never knew I had enough money under my mattress to buy and sell them.

This continued for a while. He would call me every day and we would talk for hours. I loved to hear his voice on the phone and I thought it was so cute how he wouldn't cough out loud. He said he hated being sick and coughing out loud was spreading germs in his mind. One day he didn't call. I didn't think anything of it maybe he got busy I mean he was a true Norfolk hustler and his world was the streets. He did end up calling I couldn't believe my ears when I picked up the phone and heard, "You have a collect call from" I hung up thinking the person had the wrong number.

They called again this time I listened to the name "T Gangsta"

I wasn't ready to have this type of relationship. I didn't want to be some jailbird's girl. It was cool to be his gangsta bitch, but I wasn't ready to really be T Gangsta's ride or die. I wanted a real relationship where I could touch and feel my mate. Go out to the movies, out for ice cream, the regular relationship goals. Not one I had to visit through the glass as we sat and talked on a black phone smelling of breath and *Pump it Up.* He eventually wrote me a letter because I wouldn't pick up the phone. My dad got the letter before me and tore it up. He said, "you're not talking to any jailbird, I'm not raising you to be that type of woman".

T Gangsta sent another letter this one I got before my dad. Out of all the things it said the one thing that stuck out was this nigga saying I left him. How the hell did I leave you when you were the one that went out there and robbed someone at gunpoint, not me! You picked this ruthless, gangsta life for yourself, not me! Reading that letter pissed me off so bad that I didn't bother to write him one back I typed him one back and kindly told him not to write to me anymore. The next time I heard from him again was 15 years later after he contacted me on Facebook.

There he was big as day in my inbox, in his charming way saying my name as only he could "Hello Ann" I must be honest I was excited to hear from him, however, I wasn't going to take any shit from him this go around. He repeated again that I left him for dead. I told him that I wasn't into the jailbird thing. I apologize if that's how he felt, but I wasn't doing any bids. He said he understood but what he didn't understand was why I couldn't say that to him. As much shit as I talked you think it would be easy to let him down, but my heart wouldn't let my mouth form the words to tell him. Regardless of his actions, I loved him. I gave him another chance he promised me he was a changed man.

We started a long distance relationship with me in Maryland and him in Roanoke. Things went well for a while. He was living in a transition home and working towards something better. He later was able to get his own apartment. He made it feel like a real home. He sent me pictures of his plants that he purchased. As well as the pictures of the two pit bulls he had. I quickly told him if and when I come, you have to put those mean looking dogs up. His joke to me was, I'm going to make them bite you in the ass. I was extremely happy for him and felt like this time we could really make it. I wanted us to work so I ignored the little comments from females that posted under his picture on Facebook or sent little hearts to him.

I was planning a trip to Roanoke to see him, I was so nervous to see him after all these years and excited at the same time. I went and got my hair and lashes done to look extra nice for my boo. We had planned on me moving up there if I liked the area and us starting a family. I went to the doctor for my checkup to see if I needed any help getting pregnant and she placed me on birth control to regulate my period, so there would be no issues. I called T Gangsta with the news, I didn't anticipate his response instead of him understanding where I was coming from, He went off on me. He yelled "You knew the plan, why would you get on birth control" I tried explaining to him this was for the better. He wouldn't hear it and hung up on me.

I remember crying so much that I cried my eyelashes off. I would try calling him and he would send me to voicemail. I was heartbroken. It was days before my trip and he was doing this, I would hit him up on FB and he would ignore me. I was able to get myself together, in the back of my mind how could he say he love me and do this to me. I wouldn't hear from T Gangsta again until a very familiar phone call "You have a collect call from" Yep there he was again back behind some bars. This time for Life. His temper got the best of him and when someone took something from him, he took their life. He was the same T Gangsta but I wasn't the same Ann.

I wanted more for myself, I deserved more. To my surprise I accepted his calls, they were pre-paid by him. I guess I just wanted to figure out what was going on in his head, I wanted closure. I just felt like no one took the time to help him out with his problems when he was younger. I felt very sorry for him so much potential, but instead of getting help he just acted out. I hung in there as long as I could, it just some things we aren't built for and this was one of mine. After answering calls and writing emails I vanished once again. This time I had to make up my mind to stay away. No matter how many times he had someone to try and contact me, how many times he tried to call I had to stay away.

No matter how much love I had for T Gangsta we could never be. I had to close that chapter and never open it again for edits. Which brings me to my next love, Mr. Car Wash. I had the biggest crush on the most popular guy in High School. It started off with me playing on his phone, I would prank call him every day just to hear his voice. Silly right, not if you have puppy love. I just knew I wasn't his type.

Like I said I was awkward, with connecting eyebrows and a big gap that I wasn't that proud of. He was so handsome with light skin, chinky eyes and a beautiful head of curly hair. He could dress and he smelled so good. Just so happen we were in the same school for summer school one year and that day when I prank called him he told me to meet him in between the lockers. I told him what I was wearing and he told me what he would have on.

I already knew what he looked like I had been watching him the whole time. So there I was standing there, shy and shaking like a leaf on a tree. I was waiting and waiting, I started to get a little anxious. I felt like maybe he knew who I was and he didn't want to meet me because of how I looked. As soon as I started to walk away I heard a voice yell my name "Aleathea" I froze right there. I turned slowly and there he was I swear to you there was a glow behind his head as if he was heaven sent.

He embraced me and looked me dead in my eyes, I think I fainted for a min, then came back around. I couldn't tell you our conversation after the embrace I just remember seeing his lips move. You know like in the movies how everything moves in slow motion. Yeah, it was something like that. Such kissable lips, such strong arms. I remember calling him the next day and he picked up I was so "geeked".

Maybe he did actually like me. We talked for hours then he asked me to be his girlfriend, without hesitation I said yes.

The next day he was coming in my back door while my mom and dad were sleeping in the next room. He sneaked in my back door a couple of nights. I remember us talking one night after we finished having sex, and I was getting up to go to the bathroom my dad was opening my bedroom door. I damn near died, I screamed "dad what are you doing" He quickly closed the door and said "I heard you talking to someone. I said "I was on the phone," He said "sorry" Me and Mr. Car Wash laughed about it later much later cause won't shit funny about it at the time.

I know my dad would have killed us both, bury us in the backyard with no hesitation. My dad should have caught his ass and beat his ass, cause I wasn't the only girlfriend Mr. Car Wash had. I learned through the grapevine that he had a girlfriend that went to school with him. I questioned him about it and at first, he had the typical response, "what, I don't have a girlfriend, you're my girl" I was the typical young dumb and in lust female and believed him. Until my Bestie and I did our own research and found out the truth.

Mr. Car Wash was busted he indeed had a girl. I searched his car one day and found her pic in his glove box. He was so furious at me that he yanked me out the car by

my shirt onto the pavement. Then he pulled off. Leaving me
crying in the middle of the street. Still, I wasn't angry with
him, I was angry with myself for yet again loving a liar, a
heartbreaker. Why couldn't he tell me the truth? He was
another one that had me fooled. I truly loved him. I decided
love was my problem I loved too deeply and to easily. I
trusted everything with my eyes and not my heart.

     I honestly believed that people didn't purposely hurt
you. I was terribly wrong. Mr. Car Wash and I stayed in
contact, why not the sex was great and spontaneous. I knew
deep in my heart our bond would never be the same again.
Let's fast forward a little to my friend's wedding in 2011
where I was reacquainted with Bear. I was walking down the
aisle and there he was coming up the aisle. He walked over
to me and said: "Do you remember me?"

     I said "yes" he took out his phone and said give me
your number. I put my number in his phone. He said he
had just recently come home and he was working. That he
had changed, he no longer was a drug dealer. That he
wanted a family and he wanted a wife. I thought to myself
this must be a sign, here he is at our friend's wedding
looking all good and smelling even better. I know that's what
I want someone I can build with. He said he was ready to
settle down and I was as well. He called me later that

evening. I filled him in on where I was in life, that I was a new mom, I just had my son last year.

I let him know that I didn't live in VA that I lived in MD, but I came into town often. He said that was cool. He wanted to see me before I left out of town, but I didn't want to move fast I wanted to take things slow in my mind he was the one and I didn't want to mess things up. I waited until I came back into town to see him. It was nothing but sparks when we went out to eat, we laughed at each other's jokes and genuinely had a good time to the point that we didn't want to leave each other's side. He was everything I was looking for, a hardworking man, a family man, and a praying man. He had me deep under his spell. His house would be my first stop when I came into town. I couldn't get enough of him. I can't to this day explain the electricity I felt when we were together. Yes, we had our ups and downs but I knew we would make it in the end.

I was true to him and I thought he was true to me. I gave him an option of being with someone else because I lived too far away, and he said no baby I would never do that. You're enough for me. But baby he did, he had another girl and not only did he have one she was spending time with him and his family when I wasn't around. His mom his sisters all lying to me all pretending everything was good. Smiling in my damn face knowing the truth the whole time.

I would have never found out until one night I looked through his phone and seen the text between him and his lover. Using words he and I used, "Baby" "Boo" "My Love" I was devastated. Then he lied right to my face once confronted with the information. Telling me his brother had used his phone, then his friend. I called the girl myself and she confirmed what I already knew and that was they were together. We became friends, I didn't like her one bit. I just wanted to spite him. I became friends with her, we exchanged numbers and kept in contact.

She even tried to get me a job where she worked. You should've seen his face when we both showed up at his house and we embraced each other. I even gave her a kiss on the cheek. I know he almost shit his pants. I know he didn't like that we were so close and that made it all the better for me. I came to a conclusion that we just didn't match. No matter how hard I tried it would never work, we would never work.

I loved him but never more than I loved myself. His temper was terrible and instead of bringing the best out of me, he brought the worst. He got so mad one day, then while I was driving he snatched the steering wheel out my hand causing me to almost crash, all the while my son was in his car seat in the back. That really sealed the deal that his ass had to go. Regardless of all the gifts and money it just wouldn't work. So one sunny day I packed all his shit in the car that he got for me and told him to carry his ass.

He couldn't believe I was putting him out, I couldn't either. That I had enough courage to let it all go. I gave him back his beautiful engagement ring, rose gold earrings and my birthstone ring that he gave me. Some people called me a fool for giving everything back, but I knew in my heart if I kept anything he would think there was a chance between us. I needed him to know that this door was closed, and it would never be opened again.

This love, the one I'm about to fill you in on, the one that had me going crazy and doing things that I said I would never do. Mr. Corleone. The one that I love even this very day. I met him through his cousin. It was a lovely day out, I had on a green and white sundress that hugged me in all the right places. I thought I looked pretty in my dress, well I know I did. There he was walking down the street. Fine as hell. Light skinned, tall with a beard. He had this walk that read, I'm the man. He dressed cute and I loved his unique swagger. His cousin called him over and introduced us. His cousin was like look at her butt, that thang fat. I don't know I guess I got caught up in the compliment, but I liked it. I liked the attention.

I was a new mom and hadn't had that much attention from the opposite sex. I was into my baby and being a good mommy. I turned around so he could see my butt, he responded with "yeah it is nice". I poked it out a little further for him to admire. I'm not even sure how we stayed in contact, but we did. Soon after our initial contact, we met up. Things didn't go so well so we both said we weren't going to see each other again.

I mean it was awful, I was stubborn I didn't want to comply with anything he wanted and I thought he was whack. Somehow we met up again. We both made up for the first time and then some. It was amazing whatever he did to me on that pillow top, had me hooked and wanting more. We started to see each other non-stop, I felt myself falling for him. I also felt myself waiting for him. Something I never said I would do. When we started to hang out more he started to tell me things, things that I really believed.

He said that he had a daughter but he wasn't with her mom that she lived in another state. Come to find out he had more than one daughter and the house I was dropping him off to was also a baby mother. True to myself, my love for him outweighed everything else. I wanted to be with him and I thought there was a chance for us. He would say things like "be patient babe Rome wasn't built in a day" I believed him. I didn't think he had a reason to lie to me. I guess I wanted someone in my life. I was ready to settle down and be Susie homemaker for him. But we had more ups and downs than a rollercoaster ride but each and every time I took him back.

Maybe I was crazy or maybe I was in love. He made me feel like no other man has made me feel, so I thought he was sent just for me. I loved him I thought to myself, no matter what he did or how he acted. For some reason, I always felt he deserved a second chance. He openly disrespected me and after some time I still gave him chances. Like the time we were at a friend's house and the subject of a threesome came up. I said no, out of respect for myself. One of his friends suggested that he make me in some type of way do it.

His response was "she's not my girl" I said I know that and I'm not trying to be. He then called me a bitch, and that set me off. I called him one back and that set him off. Here we were, him in the kitchen and me in the living room yelling obscenities to each other. Like neither one of us had any home training. We didn't talk for a while after that but in true fashion of our crazy love affair we made up.

Things went well for a while, not all days were bad. He truly understood me and I understood him. His intelligence attracted me. Before he had ever touched my body, he had already made love to my mind. We could sit and talk for hours about everything from the rapper Quavo to the disciple Peter. We partied all night and slept all day. At the end of our partying the same thing would happen he would always have to leave my side to go home. I brainlessly held on to what he said that he was in the middle of making a choice and I could be that choice. How pathetic could someone be to hold on to such promises? Love could be the most beautiful thing in the world or it could be the ugliest. In our case, I had both sides. It was like the more he did to me, the closer we became.

I was there for him in some of his darkest hours and he had me back in some of mine. The tug of war of our relationship became really escalated when I got the phone call that he had been shot several times. My heart dropped to my stomach, here I was all the way in the GA and I felt helpless. I prayed for him and God answered all our prayers He pulled through. When I came back to VA, I was placed on his visiting list to see him. Me and my best friend went to see him. It pained me to see him like that, this strong young man so full of life.

Now laying in a hospital bed with tubes coming from everywhere. I held back tears as I visited him. We talked for a while and then he asked me a question. He asked me to buy him some personal items. Easter was around the corner and he didn't feel like himself and he wanted some new clothes. I felt like he was trying to use me, it wasn't a new feeling I felt this a lot coming from him. I still wanted to think there was some good in him that everything he said wasn't a lie. Although at this time he never really expressed his feelings verbally.

He told me I should know how he felt by his actions. What girl doesn't want to hear I love you from time to time and if you really love the girl or just express how you feel from time to time. It would take years for him to tell me how he really felt. By the time he did the damage he and I had done to our "relationship" was irreversible, you see after Mr. Corleone asked me for the clothes, I thought he was being funny and trying to use me. I thought he was using him being shot, for a chance to get more out of me. So I did what I knew how to do, I used my body to get my revenge.

I got with his cousin. After talking with him about the incident I realized then he cared for me more than what I knew and that he loved me. This was also the time I completely understood that someone had to die. Not in the sense that I had to commit murder or suicide, but in the sense, my old way of thinking had to die. Somebody had to die and it had to be my mind, my thoughts, the old me. I had to understand that I was worth more than what I thought and I was selling myself short.

I had been selling myself short since I was five. Taking more off men than what I should. Yeah, Mr. Corleone made me realize that. After all our break ups to make ups he was the one that opened my eyes. He was also the one that is still in my heart. I guess sometimes it takes a little more time for our broken hearts to heal. I'm a grown up so I understand a love like ours is toxic. Plus trust would always be an issue because we both have been guilty of hurting each other. Intentionally going for the jugular any chance we got.

Now it's about me, no more looking for a man to fill anything in my life. I must fill my own voids in my life and heart before anyone else can. It took a while for me to get the courage to believe in myself and understand the hurt I felt as a five-year-old innocent girl, wasn't my fault. I carried this burden sun up to sun down. I eventually got myself together. Before the old me had to die, I met one more love who I thought was the greatest love of my life.

When I met this love, every pain and every fear went away. I constantly stayed in the clouds and my feet never wanted to touch the ground again. After my mom passed I found this new love and he was everything I dreamed of. I woke up to his good morning messages and went to sleep cradled by his sweet good nights. We became inseparable. I'll tell you about my new love at another time. For now let's call him, Mr. White Chocolate.

If You or Someone You Know Is in Crisis and Needs Immediate Help, call the toll-free, 24-hour hotline of the National Suicide Prevention Lifeline at 1-800-273-TALK (1-800-273-8255) to be connected to a trained counselor at a suicide crisis center nearest you.

HYPNOTIZE

By: Velvet Smith, Ed.S

Summer 1997

"Do you know what today is? It's our anniversary. Made for you and me...our anniversary..." was all I heard playing over and over in my head as I laid on my bed and stared up at the popcorn ceiling that was painted an eggshell white. I used to love this song by Tony Tone' Toni. Hell...a classmate remade it into our high school graduation song. Now I loathed the melody. I could hardly see the kernels from the tears that were streaming down my face. I didn't even think I had any more tears left to cry. Today marked a year since "it" happened. I was barely living. Just existing in a deep fog fueled by alcohol and sex. I was hypnotized by it all. Entranced, waiting for some signal to snap me back to my before life. That wasn't going to happen and this was my new normal.

Today is Tuesday, June 17, 1997. A year to the day that the essence of me was stolen. Now I lie on this bed feeling like a victim of an exorcism gone wrong. Instead of casting the demons out, the floodgate was opened to let them in. My soul was snatched out leaving me hollow and dead inside. Now I'm constantly looking for ways to feel the void but nothing works. Lord, please take this pain away. My constant unwavering prayer.

I had to get out of this house. The four walls were closing in on me. This was supposed to be "Summer of Vee". I was going to have the time of my life. Right now it seemed like I was serving life. I was a prisoner in my own body and I wanted to break free. I can't escape my thoughts. The constant replay kept me up at night. My appetite waned while my thirst increased. I needed a drink. That was the only thing that could chase the nightmares away.

Slowly, I drug myself off the bed. I staggered to my closet to find something to wear. As I lifted up my arm to put my shirt on I thought better of it. I really needed to take a shower. Although I lived in a small house, it took forever for me to get to the bathroom. I slammed the door behind me and turned the shower on full blast. I needed this hot shower to wash away the morning blues. As I stepped into the shower and the hot water beat on my body like a drum, tears poured out of me.

I was back at that day. Monday, June 17, 1996. I was so amped. I had just graduated from high school and was anticipating my new life as a college student. I had been accepted to Norfolk State University. No, I wasn't going away but I was attending an HBCU. Nothing could dull my sparkle. I was truly feeling myself. I had been invited to my

friend's graduation cookout. It was going to be held at her
cousin's house out Cavalier Manor. I thought I looked good
with my floral sundress on with these cute gold sandals that I
caught at the BOGO sale at Payless. The 1B black yaki
weave was hanging down my back, Around the Way hoops
in my ears and clear gloss popping on my lips. You couldn't
tell me anything. I was dressed to the nines. I checked in
the mirror one last time and headed out.

I hopped in my 1992 green Saturn coupe that I
nicknamed the "Green Goblin" and cruised down
Portsmouth Blvd headed to the Manor for a good time. The
cookout was all that. It seemed that everyone was there.
We were all laughing and having a good time. All of us with
positive vibes about this new chapter in our lives. The
cookout went on for hours. Around 9 o'clock I was ready to
go because I had to be to work early the next morning. I
said my goodbyes to everyone and started to make my way
to my car. Just as I clicked my seatbelt, "Kid" came running
to the car. The automatic window came down, "What's up
Kid?" "Vee, can you give me a ride home?" Kid asked.
"Sure. No problem." I said.

Kid was my friend's cousin. He always gave me an
Omar Epps vibe. Nice chocolate skin, white teeth, good
personality, and he smiled a lot. Kid always had on the

freshest clothes and shoes. He was the life of the party and all the chicks wanted to get with him. That is what turned me off about Kid. He was too much of a player. I didn't see Kid like that anyway. He was my friend's cousin. Nothing more nothing less. Playing the Good Samaritan role and giving him a ride home.

I guess I had drunk too much because by the time I pulled into the driveway at Kid's house I felt like I was going to explode. "Kid, can I use your bathroom? "Yeah" he replied. I did not think I could make it home. Plus, I had been over his house plenty of times with my Bestie so it wasn't a big deal to me. I quickly hopped out of the car and breezed pass Kid when he opened the door and headed straight for the bathroom.

When I came out of the bathroom, Kid was waiting in the hallway. "Damn Kid, you scared me I chuckled. Since when do you wait outside of bathrooms? You gotta go too?" "Nah", he said. "I was waiting for you." "For what?" I replied. Kid proceeded to tell me how he had been feeling me since I first started coming around with his cousin. Kid wanted me to stay and chill. I wasn't feeling this. I told Kid I had to go. He grabbed my arm and said no stay. I snatched away and hurried to the front door. Kid blocked my path, slammed the door, and locked the deadbolt. "Oh, shit," I thought. Kid refused to let me leave even though I begged and pleaded with him. So many thoughts began racing through my mind. I just wanted to go home.

I was standing there in Kid's living room motionless as a statue. Prayers were sent to God that this situation would not turn ugly. Kid jostled me from my prayer when he grabbed me hard and pushed me on the sofa. I asked him to stop but he didn't. Kid went in to kiss me and I moved so he missed his mark. His motions were slow because he had been drinking the entire cookout. I rolled off the sofa and made a B line for the door. Kid may have been drunk but he was swift. He latched on to my weave and pulled me down to the floor. Struggling to get up but he was twice my size and overpowered me.

I started yelling, kicking, and punching. It was not having any effect on Kid. He started laughing and saying I like it rough like that. As he had one hand around my throat, he used his other hand to unbuckle his jeans. His next move was to lift up my sundress and try to pull down my panties. I gripped my legs so tight together I thought they had melded into one. Kid easily pried open my legs even against my hard-fought resistance. My panties were down and Kid was inside of me.

That was when I had an outer body experience. I knew I was there but I willed myself to be somewhere else. Each thrust took me further and further away. A single tear rolled out my right eye as he tightened the grip around my neck as he climaxed. I prayed that it was over. Kid whispered in my ear "Did you like it?" Crickets. I just wanted to be out of there. He finally got off me and pulled up his pants. I pulled up my panties.

Kid had the nerve to ask me when I was coming around again. He said he had enjoyed my company. He crawled over the coffee table and use it as leverage to get to his feet. Kid strolled down the hallway to the bathroom. When the door closed, I quietly made my way to the door unlocked the deadbolt and raced to my car. My nerves were so rattled. I was shaking like a leaf and fumbled my keys and they fell on the floor of my car. I hurriedly picked them up and jabbed the car key into the ignition. The car was put in reverse and I sped out of Kid's driveway.

What was I going to do? Should I drive straight to the police? Should I go back to the cookout and tell them what happened? Should I go home and tell my mom what happened? Would anyone believe me? Would people think I brought this on myself? Most people would say I wanted to have sex with Kid. He was handsome and charismatic. Why would he need to take it when women would voluntarily give it up? Did he really even mean for all of this to happen? He was intoxicated. Was I prepared for the aftermath if I went to the police? Was I going to be drug through the ringer? I made a decision. I was going to go home, take a shower, and pretend this never happened.

The hot water from the shower began to get cold and I was transported back to 1997. I was always using the shower to wash away memories. The thing about it was that it never worked. It was just a fallacy. A false sense of comfort. I turned the faucet off, grabbed the towel off the hook, and wrapped it around my body. I quickly dried off and put on a pair of bright orange Bongo jeans with a rainbow tank top. My hair went into a side ponytail and my feet into flip-flops. On my nightstand were my keys and I snatched them up and headed out to drown my sorrows on the anniversary of my rape.

The local bar was calling my name. I drank continuous shots of Hennessey with Coronas as the chaser. Fortunately or unfortunately, depending on how you want to look at it, several men brought me drinks at the bar. We had great conversations and danced to music from the DJ. Since this bar was frequented by most of the people in our small city, some chicks I knew came in and we started drinking together. Later that night they were heading to the oceanfront and asked if I wanted to go. I was like sure I'm always game for a good time. I especially wanted to have all the fun I could today.

Later that evening, I returned home and changed into another outfit so that I could hit the strip at the oceanfront. Glanced over at the mirror. Pretty as a picture. The horn blew. I yelled back to my mom that I would be home later and skipped out the door. I was ready for a night of fun at the oceanfront.

* *

As I rose to try to get off the crunchy stank navy blue carpet, my head began to pound and the room spun. It was like I was in a trance. I did not know where I was or how I got there. The last conscious thought I could remember was rolling in a shiny silver Z3 BMW sitting next to a milk chocolate brother with pearly white teeth. He gave off a Tyreese vibe. We were going down to the oceanfront to enjoy the summer nightlife. I was bopping to Hypnotize by Biggie. Imitation Tyrese turned to me and sang "I can fill ya wit' real millionaire shit Escargot, my car go, one sixty, swiftly. Wreck it buy a new one..." I chimed in "Your crew run run, your crew run run." Threw my head back and let my 20-inch yaki weave blow in the wind. Now I

was the one hypnotized. The night was a blur. I could tell
that it was morning because the sun was peeking through the
mauve checkered blinds covering the sliding glass door.
"How could an entire night pass me by?" I thought.

My second attempt to get off the floor was a success.
I also found the reason for the stench. Less than an inch
from my foot was a pool of fresh vomit on the floor. Was it
mine? Was it Imitation Tyreese's? Who knew? My
pounding head and sketchy memory were proof enough that
the vomit was mine. I stumbled to the bed and it wasn't
until then that I realized that I was naked. My size 38 DD
breast was the first to flop down on the bed before the rest of
my body followed. I laid there and took everything in. I
connected the dots to arrive at my location. I was in a hotel
room at the oceanfront.

Just when I wondered what happened to Imitation
Tyrese, he stormed out the bathroom and stared down at
the vomit. He turned to me and said, "All of that drinking
finally got to you, huh?" "What drinking?" I whispered
back fearing that if I talked too loud my head would
explode. "All of the drinking...too much to count",
Imitation Tyrese sang out behind his pearly whites. "I feel
kind of responsible, so let me clean it up." Imitation Tyrese
busied himself playing maid and I racked my brain to fill in

my missing night. He won that little contest. The vomit was gone. However, my memory was still fleeting.

When he came over next to the bed and sat down I whispered: "Did we have sex?" Imitation Tyrese grinned like a Cheshire cat. "Did we?" he exclaimed. "I was hoping for another round before we have to check out." "Well that is not going to happen", I snapped back. "Why are you trying to hold out on that good pussy now?" Imitation Tyrese quipped. "It was so wet I thought I was out there in that ocean instead of in some pussy. It was good as shit." "Whateva nigga, it's not going to happen," I shouted back. "I don't even want it now with your stank breath ass. You need to go brush your teeth and wash your ass," he said sarcastically. "Fuck you!!!" I screamed and rolled over. How could I get myself into this situation?

Quite frankly, I don't even know Imitation Tyrese's real name. Where did I meet him? Did he use a condom when we had sex? This shit is the pits. How could I be laying in a bed next to a nigga I hardly knew? I guess I will take Imitation Tyrese's advice and shower. I was ready to go home and put all this bullshit behind me.

After a long hot shower, I had to put back on my funky black booty shorts and a slinky white tank top with silver sequins. Again...what was I thinking? When I looked in the mirror, my head looked like a bird's nest. What happened to my flowing weave? This was it. I had hit an all-time low. Imitation Tyrese yelled that he was going to get us some breakfast and that he would be back. Ok. I could care less.

Imitation Tyrese leaving let me be alone with my thoughts. This wasn't the first time that I had awoke from a drunken stupor to find some random guy smiling and me and talking about the great time we had. I didn't know these niggas from Adam but it was just something in me that compelled me to be with different men. Truth is I kind of knew why I did what I did. At the same time, I was in denial. Who wants to walk around some that type of label? For people to look at me differently? I'd rather be known as a whore than for them to know the truth.

The ringing of the phone jolted me from my thoughts. It was the front desk calling stating that it was time to check out. I glanced over at the clock on the nightstand. It read 11:15 A.M. Imitation Tyrese had been gone for over an hour. I told the front desk clerk that I would come down and check-out. I slid my feet into my sandals and grabbed my purse. I picked up the key, exited the room, and let the door slam behind me. The room was on the fourth floor. I wondered how we made it to the room last night. I have a severe phobia of elevators. Was I so drunk that I rode the elevator? I can't imagine Imitation Tyrese walking up four flights of steps with me. The more I thought... hell nah...he wouldn't. He just lied and said he was going to get us some breakfast and is now MIA.

I made it down the stairs and to the front desk. I checked out and sat in a single overstuffed brown chair in the lobby. I looked all around feeling lost and hopeless. What started out as fun and games have left me feeling stupid. I sunk down lower in the chair as I watched tourists shuffle back and forth across the hotel lobby floor. All of them with smiles on their faces and excitement in their eyes. I felt out of place. I knew I looked out of place. I didn't wear a smile, nor did my bloodshot eyes show excitement. I had to get out of here. I jumped up, pulled the funky black shorts from in between my legs and slid out the front door.

As soon as I walked out the door, the sun shone so brightly I had to squint and cover my eyes with my right hand. The hotel sign read "The Marjac.. Where the magic happens." Must be cuz Imitation Tyrese ass sure had disappeared. I still had the remnants of a hangover and wasn't quite prepared for the brightness and humidity. I sauntered down the street wondering what my next move would be. I didn't want to call anyone. I was too embarrassed. I didn't want anyone to know that I had made such a fool of myself. I continued to walk down the strip contemplating my next move. First, I needed to get home. Although it was only a 20-minute car drive to my house, it felt like a million miles away. How did I get so disconnected from the real me? I couldn't keep getting pissy drunk and having sex with random men for the thrill of it. Who does this? Then the answer became crystal clear. I do. Honestly, it was not for the thrill of it. This was me having sex on my own terms. No one was ever going to have power over me again like Kid did that night. The ball was always going to be in my court.

I scurried over to the nearest bench and plopped down. Rifling through my purse, I scrambled up $19.64. That was not enough to catch a cab home. Calling someone was out of the question. I guess the bus was my only option. So I go from flexing in a BMW to searching for the nearest bus stop. From sugar to shit, as my granddad would say and it sure felt like it. It took me another 15 minutes to find a bus stop. Luckily, the bus did not take long to arrive. I hopped on, paid the driver, and made a B-line for the back. I slouched down in the seat. I did not want anyone to see me. I closed my eyes and then the tears began to flow. I had no intention of crying but I guessed my body wept for my soul because consciously I was not there. Another outer body experience.

Wallowing in my tears, I knew this déjà vu moment laid squarely at my feet. How many times would I have sex with Joe Blow and regret the next morning? Hell, the next hour depending on how intoxicated I was. This was a cycle I could not keep up. This rollercoaster ride of highs and lows...peaks and valleys...to always crash and burn...and like the phoenix I rose from the ashes stronger and better. That was the lie I told myself. I knew that you couldn't play with fire and not get burned. I had the scars to prove it but I was delusional. I saw those as signs of a life well lived.

This long bus ride with four transfers gave me time to reflect. How could a young woman who appeared to have it all together be so screwed up on the inside? I had won a full scholarship to college and I had started last Fall. My freshman year I earned all A's. Behind that 4.0 average was days of wilding out, spending money as quickly as I made it, drunken stupors, and random sex with men that I hardly knew. This was followed by regret, shame, and deep depression. Sleepless nights praying to God to take the pain away. My never ceasing prayer. I used alcohol and pills to mask my pain. It was very exhausting putting on a façade to family and friends. Living this double life was beginning to take a huge toll on me. Holding on to secrets and internalizing my pain was a cross I did not want to bear anymore. I didn't know how much longer this could last.

When the bus slowed down to my stop, I had made a decision. I knew what I had to do. I trudged down the aisle and stomped off the bus. On my front porch, I struggled to put the key in the lock. Before I could coordinate the action, my mom snatched open the door. I could not get one word out before she berated me with expletives and wanted to know where I had been all night. How could I possibly tell my mother that I had been out all night drinking and having sex with a man that I didn't even know his real name? For all the love that I have for my mother, she can be overbearing at times. She can just suck the oxygen out the room and leave you there suffocating. That was how I was feeling at this moment. I was dying right before her eyes and she could not see it. Nothing I said really mattered. It was always get over it. So, I am here standing in the living room with my mother in my face and I was in a daze. Living Room. Motionless. Helpless. Flashback to the moment Kid yanked me to the floor. I closed my eyes and started singing Biggie Biggie Biggie can't you see sometimes your words just hypnotize me....I repeated this over and over as an escape. I don't even know when she stopped but somehow I made it to my room and on my bed.

Laying on my bed and staring up at the ceiling, I knew one day it would come to this. I would have to make this decision. Would anyone miss me? Had I even lived a life that was worthy of being missed? Hopelessness and despair overwhelmed me. I hopped up off of the bed and starting rifling through my nightstand drawer. I found the bottle of pain pills. This was going to take away all of my pain. I hurriedly opened the bottle and shoved all the pills down my throat and chased it with the bottle of water that was sitting on my nightstand. I laid back on the bed waiting for death to overtake me. I wanted to pray but did not believe God would hear my prayers. I tried again. Lord, please take this pain away from me. My never ceasing prayer. Tears streamed down my face. My eyelids were beginning to get heavy...I couldn't hold them up anymore. Blackness enveloped the room.

Bright lights and noise were everywhere. My throat was radiating pain. Was I in hell? I knew taking your own life was an unforgivable sin. Had I jumped from the frying pan into the fire? It wasn't until I heard the beeping of machines and the chattering of human voices that I realized that I was not dead. Not physically, anyway. Emotionally, I had been flatlined. As my eyes began to focus, I started to recognize familiar images. I saw a heart monitor, bed rail, and curtain. I must be in a hospital. I tried to scream but something was blocking my throat. I tried to reach up but my arms were strapped to the bed. I heard someone say "Calm down Miss. Everything is fine. We are trying to pump your stomach. You took an overdose of pain pills."

Later that night, the on-call psychiatrist came to visit me. He went through the standard battery of questions. My first inclination was to lie so that I could leave. However, I was informed that I was on a 72-hour hold so my lies would not make my departure any earlier. I decided at that moment that I was too tired to keep up the masquerade. I poured my soul out that night to the psychiatrist. It was the first time in a long time that I felt anything like myself. I was relieved to share my truth without judgment.

The psychiatrist ordered psychiatric testing. During my stay on the mental floor, I was interrogated and participated in group sessions. At this point, I was just going through the motions. What I really wanted to do was to get a drink. All this personal disclosure was beginning to be too much. I never wanted to go this deep. I just wanted to know why sometimes I am so happy, wilding out, drinking, and having sex and then turn around and be in a state of deep depression. I finally got my answer.

The psychiatrist came and revealed my diagnosis. I was a manic depressive. In other words, I had bipolar disorder. I also suffered from PTSD from the rape trauma. Those episodes in which I was drinking and having random sex were hypomanic episodes and the depression that followed was the lows that typically followed the highs. I did not want to accept this diagnosis. I was too smart to have a mental illness. How did this happen anyway? I was supposed to be excited to go home yet I am sitting here feeling like shit. The psychiatrist described all of the medicinal options and therapy to cope with this mental illness. I did not want to take medicine the rest of my life, nor did I want to go hang out with the psychiatrist on a weekly basis. I just wanted to be normal. I nodded my head and went along with the program. In my mind, I had my own agenda. The doctor could kick rocks.

It was not until a week later when I was taking a shower that it truly hit me. I was a young woman with a mental illness who had also been raped. I had been going through a cycle of trauma and prayed to God several times to free me. The Lord had answered my prayers but yet I was running away from what I had prayed so hard for. I was right on the edge of a breakthrough and I was really going to lose it all if I continued on this path. This had been several years of this manic lifestyle that was exacerbated by the rape. This disease was going to kill me. I had to get a grip on my life.

I stepped out of the shower, wrapped the towel around my wet body and hurried to my bedroom. I picked up the folder on my nightstand. I opened up the folder and pulled out my discharge instructions. I skimmed the paperwork until I found the psychiatrist's office number. I picked up the phone receiver and slowly punched in the numbers. I was more afraid of dialing the numbers than I was just a couple weeks ago when I shoveled an entire bottle of pills down my throat. I guess it really is harder to check in than it is to check out.

As the receptionist answered the phone, I was tempted to hang up. I mustered the courage to schedule an appointment. I scribbled down the date and time on the discharge instructions and hung up the phone. I quickly finished drying off and threw on some clothes. I pulled off the prescriptions that were attached to the discharge papers and headed out the front door.

I pulled into the parking lot of the pharmacy. I do not know why I was so nervous. I sat in the car for almost

15 minutes before I decided to go in and get my prescriptions filled. As I was waiting to get my prescriptions filled, I thought everyone knew why I was there and I believed that they were looking at me strangely. Was I going to let my mental illness continue to control my life? This paranoia had to end on some level. I continued to sit in the waiting area chair with my head down until my name was called. I paid with cash and quickly rushed out of the pharmacy.

The next few weeks blended together from black and white to a dusty grey. I was currently living in the grey area and did not know how I would ever make it back to living color. School would be starting in two weeks and I was not prepared to go and face another semester. Mostly, I was embarrassed by my prior behavior. I was known as "that girl". But I wasn't "That girl". How could I ever live down that reputation? If they only knew that being "that girl" was me trying to take control of my body instead of someone having control over my body. It seems so counterintuitive to want to have sex the way I did after being raped. However, that's how twisted and warped my thinking was. I equated being promiscuous with having power.

All of these thoughts had me going down the rabbit hole. I felt like such a failure. I even botched killing myself. I mean that's was why I was here on my bed consumed in my thoughts. Will this desperation and despair ever end?

My first meeting with the new psychiatrist was like peeling an onion. The more layers that were peeled the more I cried. It's hard dealing with yourself when you never really had. Did I even know who the true me was? Was it me in a manic state? What it me in a depressed state? Was it me in this quasi-zombie state because of the meds? Who the fuck knew? I sure didn't. I really wasn't built for all this self-reflection. I would rather avoid it and hope it would go away. I knew it wasn't so I pressed on. I went to see the psychiatrist every day for the next two weeks just so I could even pretend to be a sophomore in college. I never believed that therapy could help but it did allow me to at least be functional. As I started classes in August, I had a renewed strength. I made a conscious choice not to bow my head but to hold my head high and own my truth. I never wanted to live a lie again.

The summer of 1997 was a turning point in my life. Every time I hear Hypnotize I think about the fog I was in that summer and how I had tried to take my life because I was so out of control. I knew that it was only divine intervention that the pills I took had expired and was not as potent. That God had spoken to and revealed my pain to my mother and instead of her normal response to me it was so very motherly and supportive. I had experienced my own personal hell and I knew that I never wanted to go back there.

Do I still have struggles? Daily. Do I relive my rape trauma? Yes. There are many sleepless nights. Fearful of being alone or in certain situations with men. Bipolar disorder never goes away nor does the residual effects of trauma. I manage it with medication and therapy but I still have episodes. I just do not have peaks and valleys. It's more like rolling hills or a roller coaster at a carnival. As it stands most days I am here for the ride and those that I am not I know I have Jesus by my side to ease my fears.

If you or someone you know is in a mental health crisis, please call 911, go to the nearest emergency room, call 1-800-273-TALK (8255) to reach a 24-hour crisis center or text MHA to 741741 at the Crisis Text Line.

SKY IS THE LIMIT
BY: Dr. Jaclyn Walker

The sky is the limit always meant to me about achievements, success, reaching goals and visions until I found out it was another sky's limit to reach.

That sky's limit has to do with being high. High on cocaine, crack, heroin, dope, marijuana. You name it. You're probably thinking I get high now, don't you? Lol! Well, I don't but I've lived with an addict and when you live with an addict then you're on drugs too. Not literally, but mentally and emotionally because that's all your life consists of. Sorry, I know you were looking for a drug abuse story from me, but the only drug I've been on is love and that's the worst one there is.

June 7, 2012, is one of the best and worst days of my life. I had traveled from the 301 to the 202 to the 757 just to have some beginning of summer fun. Little did I know that this day going forward would be a peek into my hellish but heavenly future. Boy, it was like I couldn't wait to get to Ptown to party and just wild out and have fun. I mean I thought I was a catch honey, I had a gold Lexus truck, had a 3-story condo in Silver Spring with a job making damn near 6 figures, but nothing was like home especially when you had a boo or 2 there.

My BFF was driving the Lex and I was on the passenger side singing loudly my sister Beyoncé's song, Love on Top. Every time we rode down D-block, then we had to make a scene. We had the sunroof open and my bleached blonde hair down to my back blowing in the wind with my iPhone in tow, it was like my little getaway world that allowed me to be Juicy instead of Jaclyn. We rolled up on some dudes we knew in front of George's Market and gave them a ride down the street to their cousin's house. When we were dropping them off, then another skinny, light skin dude was coming out of the house. I wasn't paying him any mind because I was too busy in the imaginary world of Jackie.

My BFF speeds off and around the corner and says, "Did you see the light skin dude on the porch?" and I was like not really. She says I think you should go back and holla at him. Huh? Holla at him for what? Girl, he was cute. I think you would like him. Really? You know I gotta boyfriend, right? Whatever, I'm going back. Ok, if you say so! Then, we drive back and she rolls down the window and says I got somebody for you. He comes off the porch looking crazy and skinny and I'm like, Lawd! He sticks his head in the car on her side and starts to talk to us. He says he has heard lots about us and he wanted to know could we find him one like us. In my mind, then I'm thinking that he's really not that bad, so I told him that I would call him later if he gave me his number and he did.

That evening then I had texted my boyfriend and he was acting like a jealous jackass as usual and I was like I'm about to text Lightskin. I texted Lightskin and he told me to come through and holla at him. He told me he lived out Chesapeake with his mom, but I could pick him up and we could go talk somewhere. I picked him up and we rode to the shopping center up the street from where he lived and talked for like 3 hours. My crazy boyfriend was texting and calling and Lightskin was telling me that I didn't need all that drama in my life and he was absolutely right, but little did I know that the drama forthcoming was worse than the one I was getting at the current moment.

Months passed and I was really feeling old Lightskin because he was nice to me. Totally different from what I was used to with all the dudes before him. Still, something wasn't right. I couldn't put my hand on it, but I knew often times that his behavior was strange, but nothing that really affected me. I had been trying to move back to VA about 2 years before I met him, but this magnetic attraction to him made me want it even more. It was like we were in sync with each other and I really felt like this was my soul mate. So in November, then I was finally able to move back to the 757. I took a pay cut, but I was working on my doctorate, so eventually, I knew I would be good. Light skin moved in with my BFF and me in the 2 story townhouse that I owned back in Virginia. It was like my fairytale was coming true because I was back in VA, had a new job and I got to see my soul mate every day.

I thought my daily life was going to be 100 grand. Things were halfway decent for the most part, but the other part was not good at all. Lightskin had an extracurricular activity that he liked to do and at that time I didn't know the seriousness of it and what it entailed. He liked to indulge in what I thought was something minor, but it was really heroin. This dude that I thought was my soul mate had a dope habit. What in the world am I going to do? I googled heroin and dope and that mess has lasting effects. How did I end up in love with a heroin addict? I thought it would go away and I thought it would stop. I even tried to help him get off the drugs, but little did I know that this crap was bigger than me and him put together. I tried to mask it because it wasn't that bad or was I just that blind? He would ask me for money to pay his bills, but it wasn't that much. He told me that his body would break down or he could die if he didn't get it. I felt like I didn't have another choice, but to continue to stay by his side or he would die. I thought my positive influence would allow him to tap into his potential that I knew dwelled inside of his body. Why would this mess happen to me?

That April, I really wanted to be done with him. I was tired of living like this with him and I wanted to be done. We constantly argued and this little dream fairytale had turned into a freaking nightmare. At the end of the month, then my nephew was graduating in Georgia and I couldn't wait to go to get away from him and his bull crap. I went to Georgia and I couldn't even enjoy myself because he was constantly calling and texting me about how he needed money for cigarettes, food and even gas. I'm like you don't have a car, so why do you even need gas? This boy going to tell me that he was getting a ride to look for a job. I'm like yeah right. This badgering from him kept up over the whole weekend and he literally made me regret ever meeting him. How did my life take this tragic turn? I swore to myself that as soon as I got home, then I was done with him. That weekend flew by and I was boarding the plane back to Hell aka Home.

As soon as I got home, then he was already greeting me at the door asking about money and I'm like dag, let me get in the door. We get into the biggest argument for like 3 hours or more and then he walks out of the house and it's like 1 am. For some reason when Lightskin came home that night, then it was like a peace had come over me. I felt like a burden had been lifted off of me for some reason. It was oddly strange, but I just felt like the struggle with him was over. He apologized to me and kissed me good night.

I woke up the next day and saw it was May 7th. I'm not quite sure why the date stuck out to me, but it did. I went to work like I always did and when it was almost time to get off, then he was inboxing me through Facebook messenger about bringing him $10 for food when I got off because all his money was gone. I'm like just when I thought this mess was over, then he's already getting on my last nerve. I'm dreading the clock to strike 3 because I don't even want to go home to be bothered with him. Once my fate met reality, then I had to go home: a place that didn't feel much like one with him being there. When I get to the house, then I drop the money to him and he asks me can I take him around the corner and I said no, I have to tutor today.

When I walked out that house then I didn't know that May 7th would be another day that would change my life forever. I had gone to tutoring, but it was canceled so I told my parents that I would buy them some Captain D's. I was in the line at Captain D's and my phone was ringing and it was my BFF calling. When I picked up then it was inaudible on what she was saying. All I could make out was chase, car, and Lightskin. I was like girl, what? I can't hear you and whatever you're saying sounds crazy. She called back again and I could hear her a little clearer and this time I heard her say that Lightskin was in a high-speed chase and I was like girl, bye and I hung up. My phone rung for the third time and it was my BFF again and she was yelling and screaming saying that I needed to come to Vickie's corner store now. The 10-minute drive that it usually takes to get there, now felt like 24 hours as my stomach turned and my eyes felt swollen. It was like at that one moment then I had died a death like twice.

Once again I asked God, why me? I felt at this point that He really no longer heard me. As I pulled my car to the gas station across the street from where the police had it taped off then I knew this right here was the end of me and Lightskin. Regardless of everything this man had done to me, then I still didn't want to see him like this. I still didn't want it to end this way. As I opened my car door to get out, then I saw my BFF talking to the police and her car looking like it was going backwards into the tunnel. What the hell had really happened and why? When I got to the scene, then the police asked me who I was and I said his girlfriend. That cop looked me in the eye and said we got a 911 call about a man having a gun on Lasalle and when we tried to stop him, then he took us on a high-speed chase and he has several outstanding warrants and he's going away for a long time.

At that moment, I felt like I was having an out of body experience because I couldn't believe this was my life. My life had turned into basically a street drama from out of an urban fiction book. How the hell did the girl working on a doctorate degree become associated with this real-life episode of Cops?

As I walked back to my car with my BFF, then I was really speechless because I felt like everything that happened was my fault. I told her that I was sorry that he had done that to her car and I would help as much as I could to get it back for her. She told me that it was ok and it wasn't my fault, but she wanted to tell me that he just told her yesterday that he was wanted by the police. He told her that he didn't know how to tell me because he thought I would leave him. She told him that I wasn't a judgmental person and he just needed to be honest with me, but now everything that he wanted to tell me in private would be on the 11 o'clock news.

Anybody that knows me knows when uneasiness comes in my life then I can't be around the place where it started, so I couldn't stay at home and I had to go to my parents' house. As I'm driving there, then I didn't know what to say or do because I didn't want my parents to find out about Lightskin like this. I didn't want them to think he was a bad person because he wasn't; he just mad bad choices and lots of them. I came in their front door and I just blurted it out to them what had happened and I don't know what their response was because I was in a trance.

Maybe like an hour later, my phone was ringing and it was my BFF's number but when I said hello then it was a man's voice and it was Lightskin's brother. He told me to hold on and I heard Lightskin on the other end. I felt a million different emotions all at one time and I had a million questions to ask, but he said I can explain everything, but I just have one question before we go any further and I said what! He said I don't know what's going to happen from today, but I do know that I love you and I want to know regardless of what happens, then will you ride with me? Will you be my ride or die chick? And even after everything that I had been through with him, then I said I will ride with you until the wheels fall off.

It may sound crazy but that same peace I felt the night before I felt again as I laid down in my childhood room. The reason why I felt the peace because at that moment, then I felt like God had heard my cry. Even though he was behind bars, then it was better than him being in the outside world getting high. I felt like that whatever happened was better than how he was living recklessly. Little did I know that the next 5 years would be one hell of a love story or a love story from hell?

Even though Lightskin was in jail, then it seemed like things were getting better. In September, then I received a better job and he seemed to be in better spirits even though he was behind bars. The only thing that seemed to be going slow was his court cases and our fate on when would be together again. As time progressed, then I did everything that a good girl or now I was known as a prison wife would do. I took the stand for him three times as well as visiting every week sometimes even twice a week when allowed. Finally, our fate changed when I looked on the DOC's website and saw they updated his release date and it was June 8th

That date seemed like eons from this date, but my heart wouldn't let me leave him. For the next year, I kept money on the phone and his canteen was always full up, but I started to feel empty. I felt like that I was being seen as crazy to my family and friends because I had now dedicated my life to this man who had me in turmoil when he was out. I hated the way the correctional officers would talk to or treat me just because my boyfriend was in jail. I saw families falling apart because their loved one was behind bars. At that moment then I actually thanked God for the miscarriage I had before he got locked up because then my child would be one of the fourteen children with an incarcerated parent. I was in a pain that none of my family and friends could really understand. However, through all of the pain, then I still managed to graduate with my Doctoral degree with distinction. Therefore, I had to develop my own coping mechanisms because I had turned into a manic depressive.

What I didn't know was that God was preparing me for something greater because the pain was so unbearable. See, God knew that the PAIN of Lightskin being away from me would ignite a PASSION to create a PLAN to fulfill God's PURPOSE that was inspired by a PERSON to PROTECT his people and all of that would have me birth the LIGHTSKIN Foundation. This foundation and rehabilitative services are dedicated to inmates, convicted felons and their families that want another chance at life to stop recidivism. I never knew that God was going to do this, but of course, He did. The first things I did to birth my newfound baby was to develop a board of directors and a strategic plan with stages and phases.

See, in my mind not only did I want to create this into a ministry but an actual non-profit organization where my board and I could evoke change and when Lightskin came home, then this could be part of our legacy and even a national phenomenon. The foundation was instantly successful would have support groups, adopted families for Christmas, even partnered with another grassroots organization to bring one of the biggest Easter Egg Hunts in the 757. This foundation had now allowed me to do something positive for a situation that I was living in.

I looked at the phone one day and realized that Lightskin had like a month left to go, it was now May. I was nervous yet excited to start my life over again with a remixed version of Lightskin who would be like the one I met in 2012, but now a rehabilitated man. When we would talk on the phone, then we would always plan what we were going to do in that first week home. However, he said something that knocked me to the ground. He said you know when I get out, then I'm going to be tempted by drugs again. I said with strict conviction No, you're not because you haven't used in 3 years. He said Jackie, once an addict always an addict. I was like what does that mean. He said it means that I will have daily struggles and I will try my best to fight temptation.

At that moment, then I thought that he was crazy and didn't know what he was talking about. I said whatever, we are going to pray and that demon is not coming back. I just knew I was right, but boy I was so wrong. It seemed like that June got here like the speed of lighting because the next thing I know was I was pulling up to Saint Brides correctional facility to pick up my soul mate.

This day, June 2nd, felt like I had made it to heaven because I now had my life back. All the pieces were put together in this big puzzle of love and it felt like that for maybe 24 hours. I should have known that the first day that Lightskin was home was a premonition of how life was going to be with him. It was supposed to be all about me and him for a whole week, but that suddenly changed because on day 1, then he was having an impromptu party at our house with his family and friends. Some of which I felt like hadn't been there for him for the 3 years of pain I had to suffer, but now you get to celebrate with him while he's home. This is bull-crap is what I thought to myself. I'm like I waited all this time just to be put second all over again. Was I being selfish? Was I being petty? HELL NALL! This was my Lightskin and I shouldn't have to feel inferior to anyone.

No longer than a week later, then Lightskin comes asking me for some money and I was like for what? This can't be Deja vu because I will be damned if I go down this path again. He came up with some lame excuse that someone had given him a Percocet and he was feeling crazy. He needed to go to the ER, so that he could feel better. I said this will be the only time I will give you anything to help you because I'm done living like that with you. He said ok and took the money and left. The next couple of months seemed like I was in a re-enactment of 2013, but with less drama.

He was doing the same old dumb mess, but he had a job, so it wasn't that bad on me. But still, why was I going back on the promise that I made to myself about not dealing with this craziness. Was I becoming complacent or had I just been a sucker for love? Either way, then it was stupid and I was dumb. Smh. Finally, someone told him about the Methadone program and how that would help him. Then, the unthinkable happened while he was signing up for the program. His favorite cousin/brother died unexpectedly. Lightskin had never really lost someone this close to him and this really took a toll on him. However, he pushed through and started out at a private facility then was able to get on at the city's behavioral health office.

For about a good 2 months, then life seemed great, but halfway robotic. He would go to the Meth clinic, go to work, come home, eat dinner and go to bed. This life was bleak, but 100% better than the life I had lived before with him. But eventually like any addict then they have to test the waters. When Lightskin was taking the Meth, then it was supplying what his body needed to stay afloat, but he was no longer getting high. His mentality was still to get high and still get that euphoric feeling that he had once known, but when you've been on drugs for over half your life, then you had to do triple the amount of drugs or another drug besides dope to even get close to getting a buzz. He told me one day that he was now doing crack to fill the void of the dope that was no longer getting him to LaLa Land and back. I couldn't believe that I had a real life Frankie Limon in my house. For the next several years, then I was living in complete and utter HELL. I mean at one point, then I felt like HELL probably was a better place for me to be instead of where I was. Lightskin got kicked off the methadone program not once, but three times and each time he got kicked off, then for 2-4 weeks, it was extra hard for me to even bear the thought of even going home every day.

On top of the chaotic home life, then my work life was crazy too. The job that I once loved and raved about was starting to turn its back on me too. I felt like I had a hostile work environment with a devious coworker that was just nasty for no reason. She was a sarcastic bish that no one really secretly liked, but because she was good at certain parts of her job, then she was tolerated. I mean my life was on a downward spiral and I was ready to leave this world because I just knew God had forgotten about me. I would cry the whole way to work and contemplate suicide on a daily basis. I had plans to drive my car off the Monitor-Merrimac Bridge Tunnel and end it all due to the residual effects of the job. Here I am an intelligent woman with a professional job that she hated and a home life with Lucifer.

The only place where I found solitude and peace was through my small business and the foundation. I was going all over doing vision board parties helping people fix their life like Iyanla, but couldn't fix nothing in mine. The crazy thing is that I wasn't even trying to fix it. I was too busy trying to sweep it under the rug and hoping no one would find out. Here I am, this community leader and educator and I'm caught in a world-wind of disaster and destruction. I'm not able to pay my bills, my stuff is getting pawned and most importantly my life is being ruined all because I'm acting like it's going to get better. How the hell is it going to get better when ain't nothing changing and it's getting worse?

However, 2 bright spots did occur in my life and that was getting an amazing new job and Lightskin bought me a puppy for Christmas. See, Lightskin wasn't all bad because he would rub my back at night and aide in household tasks. It was just when those demons would overtake him that life would get out of whack. Just when I'm thinking things couldn't get any more disastrous, then they did. The next two months were like Groundhog's Day which is basically waking up to the same day every day. The sad part is that he used to tell me that he wanted to get better and he didn't want to live like this out of his mouth, but his actions remained the same.

I'm thinking how someone could say out of their mouth that they want help but turn around and do everything but get it. It was like even when he tried, then it didn't work out. He had been to the crisis center twice and that made him worse than before because they diagnosed him with being a manic depressive, but they sent him out to the streets with no help. It only gave me 2 separate vacations away from him. They claim they would put him on the list for rehab, but at this point then nothing looked good for him. He was going to end up overdosing or back in jail and that's the anxiety that I had to live with every day. I mean 99.9999999% of the time we were fighting each other, the house being destroyed and money being stolen but most importantly mental state being tested. Lightskin had done everything from selling our household products to breaking the Egyptian statues.

Every chance I got to make him feel the pain that he caused me, then I would call him every derogatory name that I could and put my hands on him too. I thought the more that I did this, then he would want to leave my house. However, this wasn't how I wanted to live or treat the man that I once was head over heels for, but I remembered "hurt" people hurt people.

Finally, I woke up on the morning of Feb 12th and said I can't do this mess anymore with him. I'm going to the courts and get an eviction notice for his tail. I'm done with this because I can't take this anymore and the court is the only way I'm getting out of this mess. If I have to deal with him for 30 more days instead of life, then it's worth it. As soon as I can leave on my lunch break then I'm going to get my freedom papers and his butt is gone. For some reason, I missed my usual lunchtime because I was doing a report and when I looked at my phone, then I had a missed call from the City. I was like, "Who in the world is calling me from there?"

When I listened to the voicemail, then tears immediately began to fall from my eyes. It was a message from Lightskin's counselor and they said they had a bed for him at the rehab center about 100 miles away. If I was in a church then I would have shouted all around that place because I finally felt like God heard me. I rushed to call him and he didn't answer, so I called his mom and told her to see if she could reach him. When I finally was able to reach him, then he was so happy and even started to cry. I just knew that this was about to be the beginning of a wonderful testimony. As soon as I got off work, then I rushed home to take him to discover when he needed to pack his bags. He went to the behavioral center and they told him that he would leave next Wednesday the 21st.

In my mind, then I'm thinking that I could do anything for the next 9 days knowing that help is finally on the way. Boy was I wrong! The next 9 days were worse than all of the years I had known him. Those days are so indescribable that Satan himself felt sorry for me. Everything that he could do those days was done. I mean one of those days he stole my whole purse with my phone and wallet, came in the house apologized and 30 minutes later stole it again. I asked God for the millionth time, Why are you doing this to me? Why are you punishing me? What did I do to deserve this treatment? I heard God say "what doesn't kill you makes you stronger" and "I give the hardest battles to the strongest soldiers."

The tears constantly running down my face could create a river and I told God that I don't want to be strong and I don't want to be a soldier. Lord, I don't want you to use me for your glory. I just want this man to leave me alone.

I'm sorry for whatever I've done in my life, but this right here is just too much. God didn't budge, I kept hearing him say you're stronger than the struggle. I mean you can't argue with God, so I had to accept His plan and His will. The night before he was due to leave, then I honestly thought he wasn't going to go because he had no clean clothes or bags packed. I was thinking that if he doesn't leave then the police is getting called because I can't do this with him one more day. Morning came and he said I'm going and he begins to pack his bags to go. I gathered clothes and personal hygiene items to help him pack.

We arrived at the location for him to board the van to go to his next location. I felt like this was the best thing for me and Lightskin. As I watched the van pull off then ironically my phone was set to shuffle and my speakers blasted,

"Sky is the limit and you know that you keep on

Just keep on pressin' on

Sky is the limit and you know that you can have

What you want, be what you want, have what you want, be what you want"

If you or someone you know has a drug addiction, then contact SAMHSA's National Helpline, 1-800-662-HELP (4357)

REFERENCES

Chapter 1:
Notorious B.I.G. featuring 112. "Miss U". Life after Death, Kay-Gee, March 1997, New York.

Chapter 2:
Notorious B.I.G. featuring Ma$e & Puff Daddy. "Mo Money Mo Problems". Life after Death, Sean Combs, and Stevie J, March 1997, New York.

Chapter 3:
Notorious B.I.G. "Nasty Boy". Life after Death, Sean Combs, and Stevie J., March 1997, New York.

Chapter 4:
Notorious B.I.G. "Somebody's Gotta Die". Life after Death, Carlos "July Six" Broady, Sean Combs, D. Dot, and Myrick, March 1997, New York.

Chapter 5:
Notorious B.I.G. "Hypnotize". Life after Death, Sean Combs, D. Dot, and Ron Lawrence, March 1997, New York.

Tony! Toni! Tone!. "Anniversary". Sons of Soul, Tony! Toni! Tone!, September 1993, California.

Chapter 6:
Notorious B.I.G. featuring 112. "Sky's the Limit". Life after Death, Kent, March 1997, New York.

RESOURCES

Book Cover: Antonio Staton of Antonio Staton Graphic Design

Photography: Jordan Janellle

Hair: Amira: Shameka Owens
      Ashley: Donna G.
      Leatha: Diane Johnson
      Velvet: Monica Holloman
      Jaclyn: Latonya Robertson

Make-Up: Amira: Sierra Shelton
      Ashley: Caitlyn Hasnain
      Leatha: Caitlyn Hasnain
      Velvet: Caitlyn Hasnain
      Jaclyn: Caitlyn Hasnain

CONTACT INFORMATION

Make sure you follow us on all social media for updates on tour dates, book signings, and media appearances.

Facebook: Gotta Story to Tell
Instagram: @gottastorytotell
Twitter: @gottastorytote1
Email: gottastorytotell@icloud.com

For booking inquiries, please contact: Amira Bethea of Amira Michele Management at amiramichelemgt@gmail.com or 757-575-6617

BOOK CLUB QUESTIONS

1.) As the reader, what did you learn from each chapter?

2.) What was your perspective on each character as they transitioned from the beginning to the end of the story?

3.) The authors use the term, "stronger than the struggle", what do you think they mean by that term and do you think it fits each chapter?

4.) Since, this is a compilation book, do you see an overall theme from each chapter and/or author?

5.) Based off of each character, who would you cast to play the main characters (Amira, Klu, Ashley, Leatha, Velvet, & Jaclyn)?

ABOUT THE AUTHORS

Amira Bethea

Amira Michele Management was birthed on the foundation of love, struggle, hope, and community. AMM was founded by Amira Bethea, a native of Brooklyn, NY who now resides in Portsmouth, VA. Amira's love for music started at a young age as a way to escape from the harsh growing pains of the African American struggle. Music was her inner peace, her therapy, and her escape to freedom.

When Amira is not working directly with the music industry or her artist, she finds time to give back to the community. She serves as Co-Chair to Believe, Pray, Overcome, a non-profit that supports other organizations through ribbon T-shirt campaign sales to raise funds for their causes, and also host different community outreach events. She also serves on the Board of the M.A.N. (Men Alleviating Negativity) Foundation as the Fundraising Chair. She has served as Entertainment Chair for Hampton Roads Pride.

Lakeesha "Klu" Atkinson

     Lakeesha Atkinson embodies many notable qualities such as being an effective communicator and an enthusiastic coordinator. Born and raised in Portsmouth, Virginia she was able to learn the ins and outs of her community and adopted a very personal connection to her peers. Despite all the odds against her, she was able to graduate from Norfolk State University.

     With a passion for giving back to her community, volunteering, and injustice, Atkinson's passion became a movement, and "Believe, Pray, Overcome" was established with a purpose of organizing philanthropic efforts. Atkinson is a board member of the Portsmouth NAACP Chapter and serves on the M.A.N. (Men Alleviating Negativity) Foundation Board. She was elected to Portsmouth School Board on November 8, 2016, becoming the youngest and first openly LGBTQ member elected.

Ashley Starling

Ashley Starling aka A. Star was born on September 5, 1987, in her hometown city of Portsmouth, VA She is the mother of two children named Amare and Ja'laya. Along with the title of being a mom, she is also Executive Director of The MAKE UP Foundation who helps young girls across Hampton Roads thru field trips, mentorships and sip n chat events hosted throughout the year. She also has a love of traveling and decided to pursue a traveling/event business called Open World Travels & Events.

When she is off from her full time as a Cardiac Monitor Tech, she serves on a few boards to include The Man Foundation which helps convicted felons get back on their feet and Portsmouth Parks and Recs Commission Board Member. An event hosted yearly called I Can Youth Brunch brings kid entrepreneurs together to help their fellow peers pursue the same dream and turn it into reality. She also serves behind the scenes at different events and always willing to help when she can.

Leatha Ballard

Being in love with writing since she could hold a pen, Leatha Ballard has been a part of a plethora of oratorical and writing competitions. She has a nurturing heart, which makes her job as a direct support professional supporting adults with intellectual disabilities, easy. Leatha sits as co-chair of the Man Foundation which is an organization close to her heart as it gives society members a second chance to make things right. She considers herself to be a follower of Christ, keeping Him first in her life.

Leatha's son, Justice is truly the beat of her heart and the inspiration for her non-profit, 4 Justice which is dedicated to "Single Queens raising Kings." When she's not writing, Leatha is honing her acting skills. Developing her original character, Sister Lollypop is one of her passions. Growing up an only child Leatha had her imagination to lean on, she still believes in her imagination to birth what others think is unimaginable.

Velvet Smith

    Velvet Smith is an educational specialist who fosters teacher capacity in reading instruction. In addition, she partnered with Dr. Jaclyn Walker to start Glamour Prestige. Glamour Prestige focuses on educational training for individuals, groups, and school districts seeking to improve their ability to reach "all" learners.

    Velvet Smith also serves as the Chairman of the Board for The M.A.N. (Men Alleviating Negativity) Foundation. The M.A.N. Foundation is a nonprofit organization that focuses on combating recidivism and supporting children who have an incarcerated parent.

    Velvet Smith has three children and a supportive mother. Her mother's strength and determination, as well as the love of her children, have always been the motivation she used to never give up. Currently, Velvet is pursuing her doctorate degree in educational leadership.

Dr. Jaclyn Walker

Dr. Jaclyn Walker AKA Dr. Diva co-owns her own consulting firm, Glamour Prestige that also has a vision board event planning/product line. The vision board event planning/product line allows her to help people from all "walks of life" set goals, dreams, and visions with family, friends or like-minded individuals through a vision board workshop. In addition, her foundation is the "M.A.N. (Men Alleviating Negativity) Foundation which is dedicated to convicted felons, inmates and their families that want to end recidivism through community events.

Dr. Walker received her bachelor's degree from Norfolk State University. She received her Master of Education degree and her Educational Specialist degree from Cambridge. She received her doctorate degree in Educational Leadership/Management from Capella University in Minnesota.